666, The Jab, & EG White,

That Is The Way It is!

666. The Jab, & EG White,

That Is The Way It Is!

Copyright © 2021

Henry Carroll Hills

Loud Cry Publishing 222
Ensley Rd., S.E.
Cleveland, TN 37323

Bible texts are from KJV unless noted

Cover Henry Carroll Hills

Bulk orders: henry.hills@gmail.com

May 1, 2021
First Edition

ISBN: 978-1-7343261-3-0

God's purposes know no haste and no delay!

Ellen G. White, Desire of Ages

Table of Contents

Inquiring Minds

As my life rushes toward its end, reality overwhelms me. The once impenetrable barrier keeping truth, blunt and honest, without any frills, in the deepest recesses of my mind has burst.

Before my beginning: While a teen, mom had a brown-eyed-hunk for a boyfriend, but her parents nixed their relationship because "he was a wild young guy" according to mom. But in 1949, at 17, mom's forbidden love urged her to marry the first guy that comes along to keep her secret safe.

It became an open family secret that mom was crazy. Her bizarre behavior intensified. When my 5th sibling was born, she would have nothing to do with him. I had always wondered why my little brown-eyed brother lived with Aunt Alice and grandfather instead of with our family. Aunt Alice told me of this incident: "Your mom stormed away in the car one day while your little brother was in the driveway. If your dad had not been close by to grab him when he did, she would have run him over."

When my elder brother, who is a little more than 2 years older than me, was about 8, he and I got into a fight as brothers sometimes do. He had me pinned on the ground by the front steps. When mom opened the door and looked down to see what was going on with the boys, it appeared to her that he was choaking me. She ran him off. He hid in the woods and would not come home even when it was time to get dad from work. When we returned home after dark, to everyone's surprise, Junior had found a way into the locked house. Dad having feared that he would have to spend the night with search parties combing the woods, was so happy that he was home safe and sound. The next day, while dad was at work, a lady from Family and Children's Services came for Junior. It was 10 years before I ever saw him again.

When I was 9, Dad vanished. He went into the corner store to get some smokes. He took such a long time. Mom left us in the car and went in to get him. He was not there.

He had walked in the front door and out the side door. She was destitute with 6 kids at home from newborn to 9. She had to farm us out to relatives. Thus, while living with dad's father, he told me that not all of my siblings were "full brothers and sisters." Twelve years later, mom's father told me, "Your mother was *loose. She had to marry your father.*"

Mom located dad 3,000 miles away in California. Our reunified family, minus Junior, moved to California. But mom and dad were touch and go. The final break came when dad agreed to do some shade-tree mechanic work. Mom tried to hide the car he was repairing in the back pasture. She drove it up to the narrow gait, but she was fearful of scratching its paint. So, at ten-years-old, I became the designated driver. It worked well until she said, "turn right" and I over did it; demolishing the right front fender. When dad saw the damage, he took his belt to mom. Her agonizing screams frightened us kids so bad that we hid in the barn. From head to foot, her black and blues marked her for years.

Mom had dad jailed. Then came the long waits in the hot car while she went to court for hours. If only her dad and mom had not dissuaded her from getting a divorce when she had the first three of us. But before grandmother died in the tornado, she had warned mom, "You'll never make it as a divorced woman with three small kids." Now twelve years into a doomed marriage, she was a broken woman with six kids in the car, an abandoned 7th, and an uncertain future.

In the crazy days that followed, dad got bail. Aunt Alice flew to California to help mom with us kids on our drive back to Massachusetts. But before we left, three kids went missing. Mom concluded that dad must have driven by the house. She reasoned that if he wanted the two brown-eye kids and my stubborn blue-eyed brother, he might as well have them. When brother was just starting to talk, he got mad about something and said, "I'm not going to talk to you anymore." For the next few years, he did not say a word to anyone. So, mom assured herself that she and I could care for the littlest two. I was in my twenties, before I was able to go west to see my dad and brothers and sister again.

Fast forward 50-years: Mom and I were watching the news. Harvey Weinstein's prosecution was the lead. Mom abruptly said, "They should hang that b..." Then she unloaded a very brief account of the secret that had driven her crazy and warped our history.

After her parents nixed her relationship with her brown-eyed hunk, she and her girlfriend, Sally, were waiting for the bus. Sally's sister saw them and said they should save their money. She knew a guy with a car, who would take them home. Since he was a friend of Sally's sister, they thought a free ride beats a bus any day. But the guy with the car and two friends turned the free ride into a gang rape.

"Sally's sister set us up. Mr. Boynton [the man at a nearby garage she explained in answer to my 'who's he?'] told us to go to the hospital. We said no and went home."

"What did your parents say?"

"I never told them. They would have killed me." Then in reply to my sympathetic comment, she added "It was brutal!" Thus, the discussion ended forever.

Before mom revealed her 70-year secret to me, the only person she had ever told was her brown-eyed hunk, who advised her to marry the first "b..." that comes along. Thus, this 17-year-old victim victimized a 19-year-old guy, who did not want to get drafted into the Korean conflict; the man that she *had to marry* because she was pregnant with Junior, the child that she abruptly abandoned years later. Her true friend, her ex-fella, had promised too always be there for her. So, when she and dad had rocky times, she would flee to her ex-hunk for consolation. After mom and dad divorced, her brown-eyed ex-hunk told me, "I could be your father."

Mom and dad both had blue eyes. Biology confirms that if brown-eyed parents have recessive genes, they can have blue-eyed kids, but blue-eyed parents like mine cannot have brown-eyed kids. Two other siblings, along with my brother that mom almost ran-down, have brown eyes. The youngest is the brother that mom had tried to give for adoption before he was born. Complications with her pregnancy led to an extended hospitalization. She argued that she could not take care of the kids that she had and the hospital bill was more than we could handle. The prospective adoptive family would pay all the hospital bills. Dad killed the notion. Years later, after I was drafted, without me around, mom could no longer handle my 10-year-old brown-eyed brother. She put him in foster care. Later in life, he had several broken relationships and has repeatedly been in and out of serious trouble.

Dad died without knowing mom's secret. He knew enough to tell his dad that not all of us kids were his. Junior can now know why mom abandoned him. Only God knows if this frightened rape victim had to marry to cover her shame or if her fear of being pregnant caused her to needlessly get pregnant to set our family tragedy in motion. After mom confided her long-held secret with me, she wanted to talk with her brown-eyed ex-fella that had promised too always be there. I tracked him down only to learn that he had died 30 years ago. Two weeks after telling me the secret that drove her crazy and wrecked so many lives, at 87, mom died in the hospital on a ventilator. Her 70 years of shame ended.

If mom's tragedy was unique, it would be sad enough. But Solomon wisely said that *there is nothing new under the sun* (cf Ecclesiastes 1:9). Mom's tragedy was but a repeat of human history with some slightly different twists and turns.

After the death of Solomon, God divided His chosen people into the northern kingdom of Israel with Judah to the south. Wicked kings quickly led Israel into apostasy, while Judah vacillated between good and bad kings, who abused the notion that they were God's *chosen*. Then came King Josiah, who "did *that which was* right in the sight of the

LORD, and walked in all the way of David his father, and turned not aside to the right hand or to the left" (2 Kings 22:2). Josiah began a revival, but it was too little, too late, to undo the wickedness that overwhelmed God's people. Josiah was killed while trying to stop Pharaoh Necho's trek across Judah enroute to fight Assyria. Four wicked kings succeeded him. Their revolt against God brought a dreadful disaster upon Judah much worse than mom's tragedy.

The Lord judged Jerusalem. Its punishment: Judah was "to be removed into all the kingdoms of the earth for *their* hurt, *to be* a reproach and a proverb, a taunt and a curse, in all places whither I shall drive them. And I will send the sword, the famine, and the pestilence, among them, till they be consumed from off the land that I gave unto them and to their fathers. The word that came to Jeremiah concerning all the people of Judah in the fourth year of Jehoiakim the son of Josiah king of Judah, that *was* the first year of Nebuchadrezzar king of Babylon" (Jeremiah 24:9-25:1).

In the third year of the reign of Jehoiakim king of Judah came Nebuchadnezzar king of Babylon unto Jerusalem, and besieged it. And the Lord gave Jehoiakim king of Judah into his hand, with part of the vessels of the house of God: Which he carried...into the treasure house of his god. And the king spake unto Ashpenaz the master of his eunuchs, that he should bring *certain* of the children of Israel, and of the king's seed, and of the princes; Children in whom *was* no blemish, but well favored, and skillful in all wisdom, and cunning in knowledge, and understanding science, and such as *had* ability in them to stand in the king's palace, and whom they might teach the learning and the tongue of the Chaldeans. And the king appointed them a daily provision of the king's meat, and of the wine which he drank: So, nourishing them three years, that at the end thereof they might stand before the king (Daniel 1:1-5).

After King Nebuchadnezzar conquered Jerusalem in 605 BC, some of its princes which included: Daniel, Hananiah, Mishael, and Azariah found themselves enslaved eunuchs in Babylon facing a moral dilemma. A food test: To obey God's dietary laws or to eat whatever was set before them at the king's whim? To obey God or the king of Babylon? Daniel, Hananiah, Mishael, and Azariah determined to be faithful to God no matter what. God blessed their commitment. The other captives from the king's seed and Jewish princes that did not see the necessity of faithfulness to God's dietary requirements are never mentioned again in Scripture.

Diet was Adam and Eve's first test as well. Such a simple test had determined the fate of the human race! By failing, Adam and Eve lost paradise and their heirs inherited untold misery. Conversely, by passing the test: Daniel, who loved God fully, acquired heaven's wisdom, good health, worldly success, and honor, as well as living to an old age.

The same test will challenge us one day. How so?

Obeying God in such a small matter as eating a healthy diet prepared Daniel and his three friends to serve God. Our obedience to God will prepare us for the events that are to come upon us in the end time.

> "As for these four children, God gave them knowledge and skill in all learning and wisdom: and Daniel had understanding in all visions and dreams." *In what manner are you fitting yourselves to co-operate with God?* "Draw nigh to God, and He will draw nigh to you" "Resist *the devil, and he will flee from you.*" Let the diet be carefully studied; it is not healthful. The various little dishes concocted for desserts are injurious instead of helpful and healthful...there should be a decided change in the preparation of food... The dishes of soft foods, the soups and liquid foods, or the free use of meat, are not the best to give healthful muscles, sound digestive organs, or clear brains... The diet question is to be studied; no one person's appetite, or tastes, or fancy, or

notion is to be followed; but there is need of great reform; for lifelong injury will surely be the result of the present manner of cooking...if this work is neglected, the mind will not be prepared to do its work, because the stomach has been treated unwisely and cannot do its work properly. Strong minds are needed. The human intellect must gain expansion and vigor and acuteness and activity. It must be taxed to do hard work, or it will become weak and inefficient. Brain power is required to think most earnestly; it must be put to the stretch to solve hard problems and master them; else the mind decreases in power and aptitude to think. The mind must invent, work, and wrestle, in order to give hardness and vigor to the intellect; and if the physical organs are not kept in the most healthful condition by substantial, nourishing food, the brain does not receive its portion of nutrition to work. Daniel understood this, and he brought himself to a plain, simple, nutritious diet, and refused the luxuries of the king's table (SpTEd 187.1).

If our appetites are not under the control of a sanctified mind, if we are not temperate in all our eating and drinking, we shall not be in a state of mental and physical soundness to study the word with a purpose to learn what saith the Scripture... The diet has much to do with the disposition to enter into temptation and commit sin (Counsels in Diet and Foods, p. 52 par. 2).

Jesus cast devils into a herd of swine (cf Matthew 8:3132; Mark 5:11-13; Luke 8:32-33). Jesus, who filled the swine with devils, also authorized Peter, "Whatsoever thou shalt bind on earth shall be bound in heaven: and whatsoever thou shalt loose on earth shall be loosed in heaven" (Matthew 16:19); then Heaven commanded Peter to unbind and eat a net full of unclean animals: He refused to obey the command to "Kill, and eat." Saying, "Not so, Lord; for I have never eaten anything that is common or unclean... This was done thrice:

and the vessel was received up again into heaven" (Acts 10:13-16). Peter did not use his Christ given authority to unbind pigs or any unclean animal for food. They remained bound when the vision ended. But some people assume that since the Church's instructions to the Gentile converts did not definitely say 'Do not eat unclean animals' that pigs and these other things have become food. Not Paul: He clearly taught that we, "cannot drink the cup of the Lord, and the cup of devils: ye cannot be partakers of the Lord's table, and of the table of devils" (1 Corinthians 10:21). When the Church commanded Gentile Christians: "Abstain from pollutions of idols, and *from* fornication, and *from* things strangled, and *from* blood," the next verse confirmed Paul's position: "For Moses of old time hath in every city them that preach him, being read in the synagogues every sabbath day" (Acts 15:20-21). Yes, abstain from idols, fornication, eating strangled animals and from eating blood, and pay attention to Moses, whose writings are preached in a church near you! The take away: The Church established Moses' teachings! There is no Scriptural justification to eat unclean animals.

Diet also attended Babylon's downfall. The king at Babylon's final orgy, learned too late that his choices had consequences. When eternity should have preoccupied his mind, he was feasting, yielding to passion, pride, and self-exaltation. If our diet does not glorify God in the Time of Trouble, our appetites will put us in mortal danger.

> Health reform is as closely related to the third angel's message as the arm to the body; but the arm cannot take the place of the body. The proclamation of the third angel's message, the commandments of God and the testimony of Jesus, is the burden of our work. The message is to be proclaimed with a loud cry, and is to go to the whole world. The presentation of health principles must be united with this message, but must not in any case be independent of it, or in any way take the place of it (Colporteur Ministry, page 138 par. 1).

Prophecy Meets History

We have also a more sure word of prophecy; whereunto ye do well that ye take heed, as unto a light that shineth in a dark place, until the day dawn, and the day star arise in your hearts: Knowing this first, that no prophecy of the scripture is of any private interpretation. For the prophecy came not in old time by the will of man: but holy men of God spake as they were moved by the Holy Ghost (2 Peter 1:19-21).

Though true, Peter's statement is problematic. For example: Consider how Abram, a holy man, who was later known as Abraham understood God's sure word of prophecy. God had testified of him, "He is a prophet" (Genesis 20:7). The word of God also defines a prophet, "If there be a prophet among you, *I* the LORD will make Myself known unto him in a vision, *and* will speak unto him in a dream" (Numbers 12:6). "Abram...the LORD <u>had spoken unto him</u>" (Genesis 12:4). "Abraham and Sarah *were* old *and* well stricken in age; *and* it ceased to be with Sarah after the manner of women" (18:11). Thus, "Abram's wife bare him no children" (16:1). But while Abram was childless, with a wife that was past childbearing, God declared, "I will make of thee a great nation" (12:2). "Abram said, Lord GOD, what wilt thou give me, seeing I go childless?" The Lord replied, "He that shall come forth out of thine own bowels shall be thine heir... And he believed in the LORD; and He counted it to him for righteousness" (15:2, 4, 6). Thus, the problem: Abraham, the prophet, who God justified because of his faith, had received a prophecy that he would be the father of a multitude, in spite of the fact that he was old and his wife was past child bearing. Hence, this holy man of God faced the stark reality that he did not understand the word of God even though God had spoken it directly to him because God's word did not align with Abraham's understanding of reality.

In Abraham's day, some men had more than one wife, and concubines. Thus, Sarai [whom God renamed as Sarah] set her servant girl up for misery as Sally's sister set-up my mom. "Sarai said unto Abram, Behold now, the LORD hath restrained me from bearing: I pray thee, go in unto my maid; it may be that I may obtain children by her" (Genesis 16:2). After, Sarai's faulty advice and Abraham's false assumption, the Lord clarified the prophecy; "God said, Sarah thy wife shall bear thee a son indeed; and thou shalt call his name Isaac: and I will establish My covenant with him for an everlasting covenant, *and* with his seed after him" (17:19). The clarification came too late to avoid the consequences.

Abraham, as the master of Hagar, honored the slave-girl with the possibility of becoming the mother of his heir. But that changed after Sarah bore Isaac. "Abraham rose up early in the morning, and took bread, and a bottle of water, and gave *it* unto Hagar...and the child, and sent her away: and she departed, and wandered in the wilderness of Beersheba... And she went, and sat her down over against *him* a good way off, as it were a bowshot: for she said, Let me not see the death of the child. And she sat over against *him*, and lift up her voice, and wept" (Genesis 21:14, 16). Hagar feared that her dreams of great honor, were to end miserably. But though God saved her life and that of Ishmael and God made Ishmael a mighty nation, Abraham's prophetic misunderstanding cursed his offspring to this very day.

Abraham's early teachings had not been without effect upon Ishmael, but the influence of his wives resulted in establishing idolatry in his family... In his latter days he repented of his evil ways and returned to his father's God, but the stamp of character given to his posterity remained. *The powerful nation descended from him were a turbulent, heathen people* (Patriarchs and Prophets, page 174 paragraph 1).

Ishmael is an ancestor of Muhammad, the Arab social and political leader that founded Islam. The liberties that Abraham took with Hagar caused their offspring that adhere to Islam to be in perpetual conflict with his Jewish offspring that came through Sarah. Thus, the promise that God prophesied, "Thy name shall be Abraham; for a father of many nations have I made thee" (17:4) has been a curse, in that, many of these nations have pitted Abraham's offspring against each other. This tragedy can be traced back to Abraham's misunderstanding of sound prophecy and his misguided attempt to fulfill God's prophetic word according to his misunderstanding. God's promise was clarified too late to prevent Abraham's private interpretation from setting those events in motion. "Sarah thy wife shall bear thee a son indeed; and thou shalt call his name Isaac: and I will establish My covenant with him for an everlasting covenant, *and* with his seed after him" (Genesis 17:19).

> And it shall come to pass, if thou shalt hearken diligently unto the voice of the LORD thy God, to observe and to do all His commandments which I command thee this day, that the LORD thy God will set thee on high above all nations of the earth: And all these blessings shall come on thee, and overtake thee, if thou shalt hearken unto the voice of the LORD thy God (Deuteronomy 28:1-2).

> Moreover, all these curses shall come upon thee, and shall pursue thee, and overtake thee, till thou be destroyed; because thou hearkenedst not unto the voice of the LORD thy God, to keep His commandments and His statutes which He commanded thee: And they shall be upon thee for a sign and for a wonder, and upon thy seed forever. Because thou servedst not the LORD thy God with joyfulness, and with gladness of heart, for the abundance of all things; therefore, shalt thou serve thine enemies which the LORD shall send against thee, in hunger, and in thirst, and in nakedness, and in want of

all things: and He shall put a yoke of iron upon thy neck, until He have destroyed thee (28:45-48).

When Isaac's posterity turned from God, He turned from them. "And now have I given all these lands into the hand of Nebuchadnezzar the king of Babylon, My servant...to serve him" (Jeremiah 27:6). God's chosen people were conquered by a heathen king, God's servant; a prophet, to whom God revealed the future by a dream for an appointed time. "The king said...I have dreamed a dream." "God hath made known to the king what shall come to pass hereafter: and the dream *is* certain, and the interpretation thereof sure." And God provided a man to interpret it: "Daniel had understanding in all visions and dreams" (Daniel 2:3, 45; 1:17).

The prophetic events related in Nebuchadnezzar's dream [Daniel 2] were of consequence to him, but the dream was taken from him in order that the wise men should not place upon it a false interpretation. *The lessons taught by the dream were given by God for those who live in our day. The inability of the wise men to tell the dream is a representation of the limitations of the wise men of the present day, who, not having wisdom and discernment from the Most High, are unable to understand the prophecies* (Youth Instructor, Nov. 24, 1903 par. 1).

Daniel's interpretation of King Nebuchadnezzar's dream initially related to the king and his dynasty. But the meaning of the book of Daniel was sealed until our day: "Daniel, shut up the words, and seal the book, *even* to the time of the end: many shall run to and fro, and knowledge shall be increased... For the words *are* closed up and sealed till the time of the end" (Daniel 12:4, 9). But in the 4th century AD, long before Daniel was unsealed in the end time, in TREATISE ON CHRIST AND ANTICHRIST, HIPPOLYTUS OF ROME explained the four kingdoms. Luther said: "Everyone agrees on this view and interpretation." Thus, while thinking that they understood Daniel, the 1611 King James Bible translators translated it while its meaning was still sealed. As Abraham's misunderstanding of God's word set events in motion, the King James Bible mistranslation of Daniel perpetuated an incomplete comprehension. This is evident by the contextual contradictions in Daniel 2: "Thou *art* this head of gold." "After thee shall arise another *kingdom*." "And in the days of these kings shall the God of heaven set up a *kingdom*" (2:38, 39, 44). In 1733, Sir Isaac Newton validated God's prophetic foreknowledge that sealed the book of Daniel in: *Observations Upon The Apocalypse Of St. John.*

The word <Strong's number 04437> *malkuw* that is translated as kingdom in Daniel 2:38 ["After thee shall arise another *kingdom*"] has been rendered *kingly throne* (in 5:20), *realm* (6:3), and *reign* (6:28). After Daniel told the king, "Thou *art* this head of gold," the translators changed the context of the prophecy from *you,* the *king,* to *his kingdom.* Instead of having Daniel 2:38 say, "After thee shall arise another *reign*" that would have maintained the context that confirmed Jeremiah's prophecy: "All nations shall serve him, and his son, and his son's son" (cf Jeremiah 27:4-11), the translators chose the *kingdom* meaning of *malkuw* that concealed the meaning of the dream as it applied to King Nebuchadnezzar. Thus, the translators reinforced God's seal upon Daniel's book until God ordained that it should be unsealed. "Since 1798 the book of Daniel has been unsealed, *knowledge of the prophecies has increased*" (The Great Controversy, page 356 paragraph 2). Here is the backstory that explains 1798:

> "Power was given unto him to continue forty and two months." And, says the prophet, "I saw one of his heads as it were wounded to death." And again, "He that leadeth into captivity shall go into captivity; he that killeth with the sword must be killed with the sword." The forty and two months are the same as the "time and times and the dividing of time," three years and a half, or 1260 days, of Daniel 7, —the time during which the papal power was to oppress God's people. This period...began with the

establishment of the papacy, A. D. 538, and terminated in 1798. At that time, when the papacy was abolished and the pope made captive by the French army, the papal power received its deadly wound, and the prediction was fulfilled, "He that leadeth into captivity shall go into captivity" (Great Controversy 1888, p. 439 paragraph 2).

The prophecies of Daniel and of John are to be understood; they interpret each other. They give to the world truths which everyone should understand. These prophecies are to be witnesses in the world. *By their fulfillment in these last days, they will explain themselves* (Pamphlet 135, page 5 paragraph 1).

1798 was the year that fulfilled the prophecy of "time and times and the dividing of time," (Daniel 7:25), which was the 42-month prophecy of Revelation 13:5. Daniel 7:25 and Revelation 13:5 were the 1260-year prophecy. When they were fulfilled, Daniel was unsealed; it began to explain itself. Pope Pius VI was jailed and other prophecies were fulfilled.

The vast empire of Rome crumbled to pieces, and from its ruins rose that mighty power, the Roman Catholic Church (YI, September 22, 1903, paragraph 6).

Whenever and wherever the Lord works in giving a genuine blessing, a counterfeit is also revealed, in order to make of none effect the true work of God. Therefore, we need to be exceedingly careful, and walk humbly before God, that we may have spiritual eyesalve that we may distinguish the working of the Holy Spirit of God from the working of that spirit that would bring in wild license and fanaticism (Review and Herald, February 6, 1894, paragraph 8).

Jesus lived for 30 years before being anointed: Likewise, the papacy gradually increased in favor with France for 30 years from 508-538. As Jesus had victory over three

temptations before beginning His ministry, the papacy's allies plucked up three Arian kings (Gesalic, Gelimer, and Witigis) to enable the pope to be anointed as a subordinate of the Roman state in 538. As Christ's ministry continued for 3.5 years/1260 days, the papacy reigned 1260 years from 538 to 1798. As much as God allowed, Christ's life and ministry was counterfeited by the papacy. As Christ was crucified and arose, the papacy received its deadly wound that was healed copying Christ's death and resurrection. A friend betrayed Jesus. Likewise, the French that had befriended the pope and had advanced his supremacy:
Betrayed Pope Pius VI when they imprisoned him in France. As Jesus was jailed on Thursday, Pius VI was jailed in 1798. Jesus died Friday. Pope Pius VI died in 1799. Jesus rested in His tomb on Sabbath. The papacy rested for the balance of 1799: There was no pope. Jesus rose Sunday, the first day of the new week: Pope Pius VII was installed in 1800, the first year of the new century, but when the papacy was resurrected it did not have the power that it had previously.

As much as God allowed, from 508 to 1800, the papacy counterfeited Christ's life, ministry, death, and resurrection. It was not until the Vatican kingdom was restored to Pope Pius XI in 1929 (the healing of the deadly wound) that the papacy more fully counterfeited Christ's resurrection. Even then, the *whole world* did not yet follow after the papacy. That part of the prophecy was fulfilled by Pope John-Paul II.

God's sealing of Daniel 2 until the time of the end hid its verification of Jeremiah's prophecy about Nebuchadnezzar's dynasty. Nebuchadnezzar, Evil-Merodach, and Belshazzar were to reign until God's judgment came upon Babylon. "All nations shall serve him, and his son, and his son's son, until the very time of his land come" (Jeremiah 27:7). Hence, when Daniel told King Nebuchadnezzar: *You are this head of gold*, this statement aligned him and his dynasty with Jeremiah's prophecy. It also foreshadows end time events. Thus, when Daniel 2:44 states, "in the days of these kings shall the God of heaven set up a kingdom, which shall never be destroyed:

and the kingdom shall not be left to other people, *but* it shall break in pieces and consume all these kingdoms, and it shall stand forever," the translators did not understand the prophetic allusion to the kings of Babylon that were to yield their kingdom to King Cyrus, who was a type of Christ.

As Cyrus dried the Euphrates, conquered Babylon, and prepared the way for the kings from the East (Persia) to reign; Christ is drying the Euphrates, preparing the way for the kings of the east, and topping end time spiritual Babylon (cf Revelation 16:12-19). In Daniel 2, when Babylon fell to Cyrus, King Nebuchadnezzar's dynasty this partially fulfilled prophecy foreshadowed Christ's eternal kingdom and reign that is the complete and final fulfillment of Daniel 2.

By the translators focusing on the kingdoms, rather than on the kings, they perpetuated the seal on Daniel 2 until our day when knowledge increased! And their understanding of Daniel 7 that they prematurely applied to Daniel 2 concealed the meaning that applied to King Nebuchadnezzar's dynasty. The meaning that they obscured foreshadows the end time meaning of the prophecy that continues to be unsealed.

Until God allowed its meaning to be revealed by the fulfillment of the prophecy, the premature understanding of Daniel 2 and 7 resulted in an interpretation that confirmed (sealed the authenticity of God's sure word) while concealing the final end time complete meaning. King Nebuchadnezzar's dynasty corresponded with the metals in the idol in Daniel 2. He was the head of gold. His son, Evil-Merodach was depicted as the silver chest and arms. The brass mid-section depicted King Neriglissar. The iron legs that extended into the feet depicted kings Nabonidus and Belshazzar, who ruled jointly. "The mingling of churchcraft and statecraft is represented by the iron and the clay" (4BC 1168.8) at the breaking up of the kingdom. The metallic idol also symbolized the kingdoms: Babylon, Medo-Persia, Greece, and Imperial and papal Rome. Daniel 2 is unsealed! It now reveals the identity of the world leaders that are living in the end time, who will be shattered at Christ's return.

Changing Interpretations

The words, "Thou art this head of gold," had made a deep impression upon the ruler's mind. [Daniel 2] Verse 38. The wise men of his realm, taking advantage of this and of his return to idolatry, proposed that he make an image similar to the one seen in his dream, and set it up where all might behold the head of gold, which had been interpreted as representing his kingdom.

Pleased with the flattering suggestion, he determined to carry it out, and to go even farther. Instead of reproducing the image as he had seen it, he would excel the original. His image should not deteriorate in value from the head to the feet, but should be entirely of gold-symbolic throughout of Babylon as an eternal, indestructible, all-powerful kingdom, which should break in pieces all other kingdoms and stand forever... representing the glory of Babylon and its magnificence and power...consecrated as an object of worship... (cf Prophets and Kings, pages 504 to 505).

"For to one is given by the Spirit the word of wisdom...to another prophecy; to another discerning of spirits... But all these worketh that one and the selfsame Spirit, dividing to every man severally as He will..." (cf 1 Corinthians 12:8-11). "The prophet that hath a dream, let him tell a dream; and he that hath My word, let him speak My word faithfully...saith the LORD" (Jeremiah 23:28). Nebuchadnezzar's dream that he faithfully told in Daniel 2, which was given to him by God and interpreted correctly by Daniel, was as true as God's prophecy that Abraham would be the father of a mighty people (the prophecy that Abraham's partial understanding altered) like King Nebuchadnezzar's worldly ambitions changed the image in his dream into one of solid gold. God's servants, who received prophecies from God were not infallible. They sometimes misunderstood the prophecies to align with their perception of reality. "When a prophet speaketh in the name of the LORD, if the thing follow not, nor come to pass, that *is* the thing which the LORD hath not spoken, *but* the prophet hath spoken it presumptuously: thou shalt not be afraid of him" (Deuteronomy 18:22).

Obviously, God spoke to Abraham, whose prophetic misunderstanding resulted in perpetual wars between his heirs. And God's revelation to Nebuchadnezzar led to the king's attempted torching of three of God's witnesses, who faithfully stood their ground for God. The presumptuous examples of Abraham and Nebuchadnezzar reveal our need for discernment from the Holy Spirit. Since these servants of God had difficulty with presumption regarding their understanding of God's sure word of prophecy that they received first hand, should we presume that we will not have to deal with presumption when we encounter Scriptures that do not align with our understanding of reality?

In the 1800's, a Baptist Minister, William Miller studied the prophecies of the newly unsealed book of Daniel. Like Abraham, Miller also misunderstood the prophecies and concluded that Christ's Advent would happen in 1843. When it did not, the date was changed to 1844. Preachers and scholars agreed with Miller's dates, but they disputed the event: No one knows the day or the hour of Christ's Coming!

> *Though no man knoweth the day nor the hour of His coming, we are instructed and required to know when it is near. We are further taught that to disregard His warning, and refuse or neglect to know when His Advent is near, will be as fatal for us, as it was for those who lived in the days of Noah not to know when the flood was coming* (Great Controversy 1888, page 370 paragraph 2).

Miller's failure to understand the event led to the Great Disappointment. More Bible study led to an increase of knowledge: *The hour of His Judgment is come* (Revelation 14:7). It had come in 1844. The event was the cleansing of

Heaven's Sanctuary: The books in heaven were opened to confirm the identity of the saints in preparation for Christ's Advent, for Christ had promised: "He that overcometh...I will not blot out his name out of the book of life, but I will confess his name before My Father, and before His angels." "And behold, I come quickly; and My reward is with Me, to give every man according as his work shall be" (Revelation 3:5; 22:12). Since Jesus had not come as predicted, many branded the corrected view of prophecy as backpedaling. The truth was rejected with comments like: "You got it wrong twice, now you are reinterpreting the prophecies. It is smoke and mirrors. You fooled me once; maybe twice, but you won't fool me again!" God's 1844 Great Awakening fizzled.

A young woman, Ellen Harmon, had believed Miller's message, and awaited Christ's Second Advent in 1843 and 1844. She was one of the disappointed. After Christ did not come, she began having visions (December 1844). She confirmed that Jesus had not come at the dates that Miller had calculated because the book of Daniel was not predicting Christ's Advent at those dates. Her visions confirmed that the Judgment Hour of the righteous dead had begun in 1844 to prepare for Christ to bring His reward with Him. Was she a charlatan? Or a prophetess that fulfilled God's word?

I [am] the LORD your God...My people shall never be ashamed. And it shall come to pass afterward, [that] I will pour out My Spirit upon all flesh; and your sons and *your daughters shall prophesy*, your old men shall dream dreams, your young men shall see visions: And also, upon the servants and *upon the handmaids in those days will I pour out My Spirit*. And I will shew wonders in the heavens and in the earth (Joel 2:27-30).

In fulfillment of this prophecy there occurred, in the year 1755, the most terrible earthquake that has ever been recorded. Though commonly known as the earthquake of Lisbon, it extended to the greater part of

Europe, Africa, and America... It pervaded an extent of not less than four million square miles...causing great destruction (Great Controversy, p. 304 paragraph 2).

In 1833, two years after Miller began to present in public the evidences of Christ's soon coming, the last of the signs appeared which were promised by the Saviour as tokens of His second advent. Said Jesus: "The stars shall fall from heaven." Matthew 24:29. And John in the Revelation declared, as he beheld in vision the scenes that should herald the day of God: "The stars of heaven fell unto the earth, even as a fig tree casteth her untimely figs, when she is shaken of a mighty wind." Revelation 6:13. This prophecy received a striking and impressive fulfillment in the great meteoric shower of November 13, 1833. That was the most extensive and wonderful display of falling stars which has ever been recorded; "the whole firmament, over all the United States, being then, for hours, in fiery commotion! No celestial phenomenon has ever occurred in this country, since its first settlement, which was viewed with such intense admiration by one class in the community, or with so much dread and alarm by another." "Its sublimity and awful beauty still linger in many minds. . . . Never did rain fall much thicker than the meteors fell toward the earth; east, west, north, and south, it was the same. In a word, the whole heavens seemed in motion. . . . The display, as described in Professor Silliman's Journal, was seen all over North America. . . . From two o'clock until broad daylight, the sky being perfectly serene and cloudless, an incessant play of dazzlingly brilliant luminosities was kept up in the whole heavens."--R. M. Devens, American Progress; or, The Great Events of the Greatest Century, ch. 28, pars. 1-5 (Ibid., p. 333 par. 1).

As God had: "a prophet", and "a prophetess" (Genesis 20:7, Judges 4:4, and cf Luke 2:36) in the past; Paul confirms: "He gave some, apostles; and some, prophets; and some, evangelists; and some, pastors and teachers... Till we all come in the unity of the faith, and of the knowledge of the Son of God" (Ephesians 4:11, 13). The church was not and is not *now in the unity of the faith*! Before the church comes to *the unity of the faith,* did God do away with apostles, prophets, or prophetesses; while keeping pastors, teachers, and evangelists? No! Is it a coincidence that Ellen Harmon's dreams and visions aligned with William Miller's study of the unsealed, i.e., the open, book of Daniel in the early 1800's that correlated with the signs and wonders that God promised to give in the end time? Faith vs presumption.

Ellen Harmon married James White. They published her writings as the *Spirit of Prophecy.* Thus, Ellen G. White wrote for 70 years (1845 to 1915). Though she is nearly unknown (you have not seen her works on Oprah's book club), she is undeniably, America's most prolific woman author. When her name came up while discussing end time events with a religion major at the non-denominational University of Tennessee at Chattanooga, this religion major told me: "You cannot study Christianity in America without coming across Ellen White." Since the encounter is inevitable, let's do it:

[White wrote] In the city of Portland, the Lord ordained me as His messenger, and here my first labors were given to the cause of present truth... After the great disappointment, the Lord revealed Himself to me in a special manner, and bade me bear His messages to His people (Review and Herald, May 18, 1911 paragraph 3).

I was asked several times, Are you a prophet? I have ever responded; I am the Lord's messenger. *I know that many have called me a prophet*, but I have made no claim to this title. My Saviour declared me to be His messenger. "Your work," He instructed me, "is to bear My word. Strange things will arise, and in your youth, I set you apart to bear the message to the erring ones, to carry the word before unbelievers, and with pen and voice to reprove from the Word actions that are not right. Exhort from the Word. I will make My Word open to you. It shall not be as a strange language. In the true eloquence of simplicity, with voice and pen, the messages that I give shall be heard from one who has never learned in the schools. My Spirit and My power shall be with you" (Review and Herald, July 26, 1906 paragraph 5).

By invitation of Brother and Sister Nichols, my sister and myself again went to Massachusetts, and made their house our home. There was in Boston and vicinity a company of fanatical persons, who held that it was a sin to labor... Sargent, Robbins, and some others, were leaders. They denounced my visions as being of the devil, because I had been shown their errors. ...While we were visiting at the house of Brother S. Nichols, Sargent and Robbins came from Boston to obtain a favor of Brother Nichols, and said they had come to have a visit, and tarry over night with him. Brother Nichols replied that he was glad they had come, for Sisters Sarah and Ellen were in the house, and he wished them to become acquainted with us. They changed their minds at once, and could not be persuaded to come into the house. Brother Nichols asked if I could relate my message in Boston, and if they would hear, and then judge. "Yes," said they, "Come into Boston next Sabbath, we would like the privilege of hearing her" (LS80 231.1).

"We accordingly designed to visit Boston, but in the evening, at the commencement of the Sabbath, while engaged in prayer, I was shown in vision that we must not go into Boston, but in an opposite direction to Randolph; that the Lord had a work for us to do there. We went to Randolph, and found a large room full collected, and among them those who said they would be pleased to hear my message in Boston. As we entered,

Robbins and Sargent looked at each other in surprise and began to groan. They had promised to meet me in Boston, but thought they would disappoint us by going to Randolph, and while we were in Boston, warn the brethren against us. They did not have much freedom. During intermission one of their number remarked that good matter would be brought out in the afternoon. Robbins told my sister that I could not have a vision where he was (Life Sketches 1880, p. 231 paragraph 2).

J. N. Loughborough wrote of this meeting at Randolph to which the Lord miraculously sent Ellen. He reported the details about this supernatural Bible study in his book, "The Great Second Advent Movement." This incredible event was God's response to skeptics, who claimed that Ellen White was not a prophet. Loughborough wrote:

Sister Ellen was taken off in vision with extraordinary manifestations, and continued talking in vision with a clear voice, which could be distinctly understood by all present, until about sundown. Sargent, Robbins, and French were much exasperated, as well as excited, to hear Sister Ellen talk in vision, which they declared was of the devil; they exhausted all their influence and bodily strength to destroy the effect of the vision. They would unite in singing very loud, and then alternately would talk and read from the Bible in a loud voice, in order that Ellen might not be heard, until their strength was exhausted. And their hands would shake so they could not read from the Bible, but amidst all this confusion and noise, Ellen's clear and shrill voice, as she talked in vision, was distinctly heard by all present. The opposition of these men continued as long as they could talk and sing, notwithstanding some of their own friends rebuked them, and requested them to stop. But said Robbins, "You are bowed to an idol: you are worshiping a golden calf."

Mr. Thayer, the owner of the house was not fully satisfied that her vision was of the devil, as Robbins declared it to be. He wanted it tested in some way. ...Mr. Thayer took a heavy, large quarto family Bible...and laid it open upon the breast of Ellen while in vision, as she was then inclined backward against the wall in the corner of the room. Immediately after the Bible was laid upon her, she arose upon her feet, and walked into the middle of the room, with the Bible open in one hand, and lifted up as high as she could reach, with her eyes steadily looking upward, declared in a solemn manner, "The inspired testimony from God," or words of the same import. And then, while the Bible was extended in one hand, and her eyes looking upward, and not on the Bible, she continued for a long time to turn over the leaves with her other hand, and place her finger upon certain passages, and correctly utter their words with a solemn voice. Many present looked at the passages where her finger was pointed, to see if she spoke them correctly, for her eyes at the same time were looking upward. Some of the passages were judgments against the wicked and blasphemers; and others were admonitions and instructions relative to our present condition" (The Great Second Advent Movement).

This meeting documents God's testimony in regard to Ellen's calling. Her Christian character, writings, and good works have blessed humanity as God intended: "I wish above all things that thou mayest prosper and be in health, even as thy soul prospereth" (3 John 1:2). She exalted Jesus thru sound Bible teachings, promoted education globally, taught sound health principles, established hospitals like Loma Linda, and taught folks how to better themselves. Google her. Critics may belittle her, but they cannot fault her godly life and character: "Whereas they speak against you as evildoers, they may by your good works, which they shall behold, glorify God in the day of visitation" (1 Peter 2:12).

God's Timing

After King Nebuchadnezzar altered the meaning of the Dream that he had had in Daniel 2, God gave him a second dream. This dream expanded and explained his first dream as noted in this partial comparison.

Metal Idol (Daniel 2)	Great Tree (Daniel 4)
A great image (2:31)	Height to heaven (4:11 & 20)
Thou art this head (2:38)	The tree is you (4:20-22)
This head (2:38) [man's thought center]	Tree's heart (4:16) [cf Proverbs 23:7]
The beasts (2:38) given into thine hand	The beasts (4:12 & 21) had shadow under it
You are a king (2:21 & 37) for the God of heaven hath given thee a kingdom	Most High rules (4:17 & 22) the Kingdom of men, and giveth it to whomsoever He will
Belly & thighs (2:32-33,39-40) of brass and iron	The stump (4:15) Band of iron and brass
Stone destroyed it (2:34, 45)	Hew down the tree (4:13-14, 23)
The great God (2:45) has made known to the king what shall come...hereafter: and the dream is certain and the interpretation thereof sure	The interpretation (4:24) O king, and this is the decree of the Most High which is come upon my lord the king
The God of heaven will (2:44) set up a kingdom, the kingdom shall stand for ever	Thy kingdom (4:26) is sure unto thee, the heavens do rule

The 1611 King James translators' inconsistencies like prematurely focusing Daniel 2 on the kingdom and focusing Daniel 4 on the king to the neglect of his kingdom, were used of God to keep Daniel sealed until after 1798. But when knowledge increased and Daniel was unsealed and opened, the KJV obscured its end time meaning. The head of gold in the first dream that they linked to the kingdom of Babylon was also the great tree in the second dream that they should also have linked to the kingdom of Babylon.

In Daniel 2, like Daniel 4, the prophecy initially related to King Nebuchadnezzar's dynasty that was destroyed by Cyrus, who was symbolic of Christ and thus, the Persian Empire foreshadowed Christ's eternal kingdom. Had the translators understood the local application of Daniel 2, its dual meaning about the king and his kingdom would have been conveyed. But the primary focus on the great kingdoms from Babylon to Rome that they prematurely understood from studying Daniel 7 concealed the meaning that related to the king's dynasty. Not long after 1798, before knowledge had increased very much, White confirmed that "The Holy Spirit represents worldly kingdoms under the symbol of fierce beasts of prey" (Christ's Object Lessons, p. 77 par. 1). As Daniel 2 gave an outline of the world's history from Nebuchadnezzar's dynasty thru the mighty kingdoms from Babylon to Rome until Christ Coming, Daniel 4 is not limited to the king of Babylon. It reveals truth about his kingdom, Babylon, and it reveals details about the timeline that aligns with end time events. The timing in Daniel 4 ("let seven times pass over him" 4:16) is initially 7-years "according to their *appointed* time every year" (Esther 9:27). "Seven times shall pass over thee, till thou know that the Most High ruleth in the kingdom of men, and giveth it to whomsoever He will" (Daniel 4:25). When the 7-times ended, it had been 7-years. They were: The end of the days. *"At the end of the days*, I Nebuchadnezzar lifted up mine eyes unto heaven, and mine understanding returned unto me, and I blessed the Most High, and I praised and honored Him" (4:34). The term *times* was interchanged with days that were *years*. In Scriptures, a day can symbolize a year: "Each day for a year" (Ezekiel 4:6). Since a day, a year, and a time are interchangeable, in Bible prophecy, the context of the Scriptures are important to understand the timing. To further complicate Bible study, the symbolism is not limited to a time being a day or a year. David states of yesterday, "A thousand years in Thy sight are but as yesterday" (Psalms 90:4). Peter explains that David's thousand year *yesterday* is a *day*: "Be not ignorant of this one thing, that one day is with the Lord as a thousand years, and a thousand years as one day" (2 Peter 3:8). From this, it is obvious that the calculation goes both ways: A day can depict a thousand years, and a thousand years a day, i.e., *the end of the days* (7-years) in Daniel 4 is prophetically also *the end of the 7-thousands years* allotted to Babylon.

Babylon refers to the ancient kingdom and "The term Babylon, derived from Babel, and signifying confusion, is applied in Scripture to the various forms of false or apostate religion" (Spirit of Prophecy Volume 4, page 232 par. 2). Symbolically, all false and apostate religions are Babylon.

The prophet Isaiah also identifies the king of Babylon as Lucifer, i.e., Satan: "Take up this proverb against the king of Babylon, and say... How art thou fallen from heaven, O Lucifer" (Isaiah 14:4, 12). Since Daniel 4 reveals that the king of Babylon was to have 7-years of insanity, it is also revealing that Satan's insanity is to last for 7,000-years. This is the context: Sin's duration is limited to six thousand years and its destruction comes at the end of the seventh thousand-year sabbath. According to White, "The great controversy between Christ and Satan that has been carried forward for nearly six thousand years is soon to close." From the future perspective of the redeemed in heaven, White explains: "Satan's work of ruin is forever ended. *For six thousand years he has wrought his will...* The whole earth is at rest..." (Great Controversy 1888, p. 518.1, 673.2).

A contemporary of White, Crosier, put it this way: "The last act of deliverance will be at the end of the 1000 years" which is at the end of "the great Sabbath, *the seventh millennium*; Hebrews 4:3" (www.sdadefend.com). And White affirmed his observation: "Brother *Crosier had the true light...* in the Day-Star, Extra, February 7, 1846. *I feel fully authorized by the Lord, to recommend that Extra, to every saint*" (Word to the Little Flock, page 12 paragraph 8). This conclusion about the 7th millennium is based on Bible study.

And he laid hold on the dragon, that old serpent, which is the Devil, and Satan, and bound him a thousand years... And when the thousand years are expired, Satan shall be loosed out of his prison (cf Revelation 20:3, 6-7).

The word of God covers a period of history reaching from the creation to the coming of the Son of man in the clouds of heaven... Through all these centuries the truth of God has remained the same. That which was truth in the beginning is truth now. Although new and important truths appropriate for succeeding generations have been opened to the understanding, *the present revealings do not contradict those of the past. Every new truth understood only makes more significant the old* (Review and Herald, March 2, 1886 paragraph 6).

Satan, the king of Babylon, is allowed to tempt the people on earth for 6,000-years, then he receives a deadly wound, i.e., he is bound for 1,000-years, and after that time has elapsed, he is released for an appointed time. An apostate church, Babylon, i.e., the papacy, has been allowed to reign for 1260-years. Then, like Satan, the king of Babylon received a deadly wound, which was eventually healed, and the kingdom was restored to the pope for an appointed time.

All that God has in prophetic history specified to be fulfilled in the past has been, and all that is yet to come in its order will be. Daniel, God's prophet, stands in his place. John stands in his place. In the Revelation, the

Lion of the tribe of Judah has opened to the students of prophecy the book of Daniel, and thus is Daniel standing in his place. He bears his testimony, that which the Lord revealed to him in vision of the great and solemn events which we must know as we stand on the very threshold of their fulfillment (Manuscript Release Vol. 17, p. 10).

Historical events, showing the direct fulfillment of prophecy, were set before the people, and the prophecy was seen to be a figurative delineation of events leading down to the close of this earth's history... The people now have a special message to give to the world... (Ibid., p. 1).

Though it is not specified in Daniel 2, the truth in Daniel 4, expands and explains: Before the idol is crushed, papal Babylon receives its deadly wound that is healed before Christ Comes. When do the 6,000 years end? Ussher's chronology has the earth older; the Hebrew Calendar aligns 2021 with the year 5781, which places the end of the 6,000 years hundreds of years in the future; and Gregory Lang ends them in 2027. But Miller's Bible study has revealed that *the Hour of His Judgment began in 1844*, which predisposes the question: How long is *the Hour of His Judgment?*

Judgment is first mentioned in the creation story when God created time: "Evening and the morning...the first day" (Genesis 1:5). After establishing a day in Literal Time, God told Adam "In the *day* that thou eatest thereof thou shalt surely die" (2:17). But Adam did not die in Literal Time, i.e., the literal day that he sinned. "All the days that Adam lived were nine hundred and thirty years: *and he died*" (5:5). And Adam did not die in *long time*, *"each day for a year"* (Ezekiel 4:6), i.e., the year he sinned. Adam died in *Millennial Time*, i.e., in the day/1,000 years that he sinned.

Remembering Peter's caution: Do not be ignorant of God's timing (a day with God is like 1,000 years or 1,000 years is like a day), and since God's judgment of Adam aligned with God's timing, i.e., *Millennial Time*, the same is undoubtedly true of God's Judgment Hour as it relates to sin that is limited to 7,000 years: 6,000 years for Satan to tempt us, and 1,000 years for the earth to have its Sabbath rest.

From William Miller's study, the Judgment Hour of the dead began 22 October 1844. "Judgment must begin at the house of God" (1 Peter 4:17) viz. the Roman Catholic Church. It is written, "Of the church in Sardis...thou hast a name that thou livest, and art dead (Revelation 3:1). Babylon, e.g., the Roman Catholic Church, fulfilled the prophecy when it died in 1798; it was the dead Church that Jesus called Sardis. It was still dead 22 October 1844 at which time "The Saviour did enter the Most Holy Place in 1844 to cleanse the sanctuary and the investigative judgment had commenced for the dead" (Manuscript Release Vol. 10, p. 269 par. 1).

"Moses sat to judge the people...from the morning unto the evening" (Exodus 18:13).

Under the Mosaic system the cleansing of the sanctuary, or the great Day of Atonement, occurred on the tenth day of the seventh Jewish month (Leviticus 16:29-34) (Great Controversy, page 399 paragraph 4).

That same Day: for it is a Day of Atonement (Leviticus 23:27).

In the day when God shall judge the secrets of men by Jesus Christ (Romans 2:16).

On the Day of Atonement, the High Priest ministered in the Sanctuary during the daylight hours: *From morning to evening.* And Jesus clarified the length of a daylight hour: "Are there not twelve hours in the day?" (John 11:9). *The length of an hour being determined by the length of the day is a Jewish principle called* <u>*Sha'ah*</u> <u>*Zemanit*</u>: "*Proportional hour... Total daylight hours divided by 12*" (www.chabad.org).

Fear God, and give glory to Him; for *the hour of His Judgment is Come*: And worship Him that made heaven, and earth, and the sea, and the fountains of waters (Revelation 14:7).

How long is a Judgment HOUR? A literal hour is 60 minutes. In prophecies that use a day for a year, an hour can be a month (1/12th of a 360 day/prophetic year = 30 days). An hour is 15 days based on a 24-hour day in a 360day/prophetic year. Two years before the fall of the Ottoman Empire, Josiah Litch used 1/24th of a day to precisely calculate that event that is foretold in Revelation 9. Based on Adam's *Millennial Judgment* and the fact that the Temple's Day of Atonement services took place during the daylight hours: The length of a *Judgment Hour* is *1/12th of a 1000year day*, which is *83 years and 4 months*.

An HOUR (cf Strong)

A certain definite time
The daytime
A twelfth part of the day-time, an hour
Any definite time, point of time, moment

The Judgment HOUR of the dead Roman Catholic Church confirms the length of a judgment Hour as 83 years 4 months. It received its deadly wound in 1798. It remained dead for the 83 years 4 months from October 22, 1844 until February 22, 1928. When the time allotted for the Judgment Hour of the dead ended, there was a brief tarrying time in which the papacy's deadly wound was healed by Mussolini, who restored a secular kingdom to Pope Pius XI via the Lateran Treaty. "The vision is yet for an appointed time, but at the end it shall speak, and not lie: though it tarry, wait for it...it will surely come, it will not tarry" (Habakkuk 2:3). After the Judgment Hour of the dead Roman Church ended in 1928, the tarrying time followed, and the healing of its deadly wound began in February 1929. The deadly wound was healed by June 1929. As the Judgment of the dead Roman Church began on the October 22 Day of Atonement in 1844, the 83-year 4-month Judgment of the living Roman Church began on the 1929 Day of Atonement, which was on October 14. Thus, the Roman Church had 7-heads/popes that ruled from October 14, 1929 until February 14, 2013, at which time Pope Benedict XVI resigned in the midst of the priests' fornication scandal. He was the 7th solo pope/head to rule the papacy in fulfillment of Revelation 13:1-10. When he resigned, papal Babylon, was transformed into a dual monarchy with two living popes (Benedict Emeritus and Francis I). As ancient Babylon had two kings at the time that it fell, so it is today: "Babylon is fallen is fallen...because...of her fornication" "Babylon the great is fallen...the kings of the earth have committed fornication with her... Come out of her, My people, that ye be not partakers of her sins, and that ye receive not of her plagues" (Revelation 14:8; 18:2-4).

The seven solo popes/kings that ruled during the Judgment Hour of the living were: Popes Pius XI & XII, John XXIII, Paul VI, John-Paul I & II, and Benedict XVI. Each hour allotted to judge the dead and the living has aligned with an 83-year 4-month Judgment Hour. They have ended! God's books in heaven are current. We are in the final sealing time.

Satan is now using every device in this sealing time to keep the minds of God's people from the present truth and to cause them to waver. I saw a covering that God was drawing over His people to protect them in the time of trouble; and every soul that was decided on the truth and was pure in heart was to be covered with the covering of the Almighty (Early Writings, page 43 paragraph 2).

The Judgment

"The Lord God will do nothing, but He revealeth His secret unto His servants the prophets." "The secret things belong unto the Lord our God, but those things which are revealed belong unto us and to our children forever" (Amos 3:7; Deuteronomy 29:29).

In his pride and arrogancy, with a reckless feeling of security Belshazzar "made *a great feast* to a thousand of his lords, and drank wine before the thousand." All the attractions that wealth and power could command, added splendor to the scene. Beautiful women with their enchantments were among the guests in attendance at the royal banquet. Men of genius and education were there. Princes and statesmen drank wine like water and reveled under its maddening influence.

With reason dethroned through shameless intoxication, and with lower impulses and passions now in the ascendancy, the king himself took the lead in the riotous orgy. As the feast progressed, he "commanded to bring the golden and silver vessels which... Nebuchadnezzar had taken out of the temple which was in Jerusalem; that the king, and his princes, his wives, and his concubines, might drink therein." The king would prove that nothing was too sacred for his hands to handle. "They brought the golden vessels...and the king, and his princes, his wives, and his concubines, drank in them. They drank wine, and praised the gods of gold, and of silver, of brass, of iron, of wood, and of stone" (Prophets and Kings, p. 523).

God has permitted the light of health reform to shine upon us in these last days, that by walking in the light we may escape many of the dangers to which we shall be exposed. Satan is working with great power to lead men to indulge appetite, gratify inclination, and spend their days in heedless folly. He presents attractions in a life of selfish enjoyment and of sensual indulgence. Intemperance saps the energies of both mind and body. He who is thus overcome has placed himself upon Satan's ground, where he will be tempted and annoyed, and finally controlled at pleasure by the enemy of all righteousness. Parents need to be impressed with their obligation to give to the world children having well-developed characters, --children who will have moral power to resist temptation, and whose life will be an honor to God and a blessing to their fellowmen. Those who enter upon active life with firm principles, will be prepared to stand unsullied amid the moral pollutions of this corrupt age. Let mothers improve every opportunity to educate their children for usefulness (CE 175.3).

The prophet first reminded Belshazzar of matters with which he was familiar, but which had not taught him the lesson of humility that might have saved him. He spoke of Nebuchadnezzar's sin and fall, and of the Lord's dealings with him--the dominion and glory bestowed upon him, the divine judgment for his pride, and his subsequent acknowledgment of the power and mercy of the God of Israel; and then in bold and emphatic words he rebuked Belshazzar for his great wickedness. He held the king's sin up before him, showing him the lessons, he might have learned but did not. Belshazzar had not read aright the experience of his grandfather, nor heeded the warning of events so significant to himself. The opportunity of knowing and obeying the true God had been given him, but had not been taken to heart, and he was about to reap the consequence of his rebellion (Prophets and Kings, page 529 paragraph 2).

In the history of Nebuchadnezzar and Belshazzar, God speaks to the people of today. *The condemnation* *that will fall upon the inhabitants of the earth in this day will be because of **their rejection of light**. Our condemnation in the judgment will not result from the fact that we have lived in error, but from the fact that we have neglected Heaven-sent opportunities for discovering truth.* The means of becoming conversant with the truth are within the reach of all; but, like the indulgent, selfish king, we give more attention to the things that charm the ear, and please the eye, and gratify the palate, than to the things that enrich the mind, the divine treasures of truth. It is through the truth that we may answer the great question, "What must I do to be saved?" (Bible Echo, September 17, 1894, paragraph 5).

As it was in the days of Noe, so shall it be also in the days of the Son of man (Luke 17:26).

The days before the Flood steal silently on as a thief in the night. Noah is now making his last effort in warnings, entreaty, and appeal to the rejecters of God's message. With tearful eye, trembling lip, and quivering voice he makes his last entreaty for them to believe and secure a refuge in the ark. But they turn from him with impatience and contempt that he should be so egotistical as to suppose his family are the only ones right in the vast population of the earth. They have no patience with his warnings, with his strange work of building an immense boat on dry ground. Noah, they said, was insane.

Reason, science, and philosophy assured them Noah was a fanatic. None of the wise men and honored of the earth believed the testimony of Noah. If these great men were at ease and had no fears, why should they be troubled? (Manuscript Release Vol. 10, p. 374).

The Spirit of God is departing from many among His people. Many have entered into dark, secret paths, and some will never return. They will continue to stumble to their ruin. They have tempted God; **they have rejected light**. All the evidence that will ever be given them they have received, and have not heeded. They have chosen darkness rather than light, and have defiled their souls... The world is polluted, corrupted, as was the world in the days of Noah. The only remedy is belief in the truth, acceptance of the light. Yet many have listened to the truth spoken in demonstration of the Spirit, and they have not only refused to accept the message, but they have hated the light. These men are parties to the ruin of souls. They have interposed themselves between the heaven-sent light and the people (Pamphlet 154, p. 34).

The righteous and the wicked will still be living upon the earth in their mortal state—men will be planting and building, eating and drinking, all unconscious that the final, irrevocable decision has been pronounced in the sanctuary above. Before the flood, after Noah entered the ark, God shut him in, and shut the ungodly out; but for seven days the people, knowing not that their doom was fixed, continued their careless, pleasure-loving life, and mocked the warnings of impending judgment. "So," says the Saviour, "shall also the coming of the Son of man be" [Matthew 24:39.] Silently, unnoticed as the midnight thief, will come the decisive hour which marks the fixing of every man's destiny, the final withdrawal of mercy's offer to guilty men (Great Controversy 1888, 491.2).

In Noah's Day, he knew when to go into the ark! From September 2011 thru September 2012, based on my study of Revelation 17, I tweeted eight times that Pope Benedict XVI would not be pope after the spring of 2013 (see Twitter's archives). He was the pope that was to reign a *short space*. Five of the kings/popes/heads that had been restored thru the 1929 Lateran Treaty were fallen, i.e., dead ("their lord [was] *fallen* down *dead*" Judges 3:25). When the prophecy met history: Popes Pius XI & XII, John XXIII, Paul VI, and John-Paul I were dead. John-Paul II is the pope, i.e., the *one that is*. The one that is to reign for a short space (Revelation 17:10), was Benedict. *"The number 7 indicates completeness, and is symbolic of the fact that **the messages extend to the end of time**, while the symbols used reveal the condition of the church at different periods in the history of the world"* (Acts of the Apostles, p. 585 par. 3). By Babylonian reckoning, Pope Benedict XVI's reign began March 29, 2006. He resigned effective February 28, 2013, a month and a day short of seven years, i.e., *a short space*. As it was in the Days of Noah (he was in the ark for 7-days before the rain began), counting a day in prophecy as a year: Seven years after Benedict XVI resigned; on February 14, 2020, two hurricanes merged in the North Atlantic Ocean that formed a bomb cyclone that struck Iceland, England, and Europe. That very day, the World Health Organization declared COVID-19 a global pandemic. COVID-19 is a judgment from God just as sure as the flood in Noah's Day! "First, I will recompense their iniquity and their sin double" (Jeremiah 16:18). "Babylon is fallen, is fallen." The end is near: The doubling of the seven years will end February 14, 2027.

Each period of the fulfillment of prophetic history is a preparation for the advanced light which will succeed each period. As the prophecy comes to an end, there is to be a perfect whole (Manuscript Release Vol. 13, p. 15).

Why, then, this widespread ignorance concerning an important part of Holy Writ? Why this general reluctance to investigate its teachings? It is the result of a studied effort of the prince of darkness to conceal from men that which reveals his deceptions. For this reason, Christ the Revelator, foreseeing the warfare that would be waged against the study of the Revelation, pronounced a blessing upon all who should read, hear, and observe the words of the prophecy (Great Controversy 1888, p. 342).

Great truths that have lain unheeded and unseen... are to shine from God's word in their native purity. To those who truly love God the Holy Spirit will reveal truths that have faded from the mind, and will also reveal truths that are entirely new. **Those who eat the flesh and drink the blood of the Son of God will bring from the books of Daniel and Revelation truth that is inspired by the Holy Spirit.** *They will start into action forces that cannot be repressed* (RH, August 17, 1897, par. 19).

In your study of the word of God, penetrate deeper and still deeper beneath the surface. *Lay hold by faith on divine power* and sound the depths of inspiration (Testimonies Vol. 9, page 151 paragraph 1).

Every child of God should be intelligent in the Scriptures, and able, *by tracing the fulfillment of prophecy, to show our position in this world's history* (Review and Herald January 27, 1885, paragraph 7).

If the Bible student learns from the great Teacher who inspired Bible history, he will know the truth... *History and prophecy testify that the God of the whole earth revealeth secrets through His chosen light-bearers to the world* (Manuscript Release Vol. 3, p. 186 par. 2).

These predictions of the Infinite One, recorded on the prophetic page and traced on the pages of history, were given to demonstrate that God is the ruling power in the affairs of this world. He changes the times and the seasons, He removes kings and sets up kings, to fulfill His own purpose (YI, September 29, 1903, par. 3).

We who are living in this age have greater light and privileges than were given to Abraham, Joseph, Moses, Daniel, Ezra, Nehemiah, and other ancient worthies, and we are under correspondingly greater obligation to let our light shine to the world. God has made us the depositaries of His law. We have been redeemed by the precious blood of Christ, and we are to follow in His footsteps, to represent Him before the world. But *are we faithful depositaries of the truth, correctly representing it amid the spiritual declension and moral corruption that now exist?* Are we doing all that we might and should do to diffuse the precious light of truth? Brethren, you see the truth, you understand the claims of God's law; you know that no willful transgressor will enter into life, and yet you see that law made void in the world. What is your duty? You are not to ask, "What is convenient for me? What is agreeable?" but, "What can I do to save souls?" (Gospel Workers 1892, p. 434.1).

Even the prophets who were favored with the special illumination of the Spirit did not fully comprehend the import of the revelations committed to them. The meaning was to be unfolded from age to age, as the people of God should need the instruction therein contained (Great Controversy 1888, page 344 paragraph 1).

The Revelation is the supplement of Daniel... *These messages were given, not for those that uttered the prophecies, but for us who are living amid the scenes of their fulfillment* (Manuscript Release Vol. 17, p. 19.1).

Study Revelation in connection with Daniel; for history will be repeated (EGW 1888 Materials, p. 1491 par. 1).

God designed that the discovery of these things... establish the faith of men in *inspired history* (1SP 90.1).

History has been and will be repeated. [But] There will always be those who, though apparently conscientious, will grasp at the shadow, preferring it to the substance. They take error in the place of truth... (Review and Herald, February 5, 1901, par. 5).

I saw the necessity of the messengers, especially, watching and checking all fanaticism wherever they might see it rise. Satan is pressing in on every side, and unless we watch for him, and have our eyes open to his devices and snares, and have on the whole armor of God, the fiery darts of the wicked will hit us. *There are many precious truths contained in the Word of God, but it is "present truth" that the flock needs now. I have seen the danger of the messengers running off from the important points of present truth, to dwell upon subjects that are not calculated to unite the flock and sanctify the soul. Satan will here take every possible advantage to injure the cause* (Early Writings, page 63 paragraph 1).

When Ancient Babylon fell, it had 2 kings. The judgment of Belshazzar was swift and unexpected. When he saw the writing on the wall, it was too late. Papal Babylon with two popes has been identified by its priests' fornication. "Come out of her My people." The Mark of the Beast will separate God's people from the worldly before Judgment is dispensed!

"And he causeth all, both small and great, rich and poor, free and bond, to receive a mark in their right hand, or in their foreheads and that no man might buy or sell, save he that had the mark, or the name of the beast, or the number of his name" (1888 Materials, p. 700.2).

This is the test that the people of God must have before they are sealed. All who prove their loyalty to God by observing His law, and refusing to accept a spurious Sabbath, will rank under the banner of the Lord God Jehovah, and will receive the seal of the living God. Those who yield the truth of heavenly origin, and accept the Sunday Sabbath, will receive the Mark of the Beast. What need will there be of the solemn warning not to receive the Mark of the Beast, when all the saints of God are sealed and ticketed for the New Jerusalem? "O consistency, thou art a jewel!" (1888 Materials, p. 701.1).

Worship

"Satan sought to make Daniel's faithfulness to God the cause of his destruction" (Signs of the Times, November 4, 1886, par. 2). But "Did Daniel cease to pray because this decree was to go into force? —No, that was just the time when he needed to pray" (RH, May 3, 1892, par. 11).

The decree goes forth from the king. Daniel is acquainted with the purpose of his enemies to ruin him. But he does not change his course in a single particular. With calmness he performs his accustomed duties, and at the hour of prayer he goes to his chamber, and with his windows open toward Jerusalem, he offers his petitions to the God of heaven. By his course of action, he fearlessly declares that no earthly power has the right to come between him and his God and tell him to whom he should or should not pray. Noble man of principle! He stands before the world today a praiseworthy example of Christian boldness and fidelity. He turns to God with all his heart, although he knows that death is the penalty for his devotion (The Sanctified Life, p. 43 par. 3).

Daniel was a man of prayer; and God gave him wisdom and firmness to resist every influence that conspired to draw him into the snare of intemperance. Even in his youth he was a moral giant in the strength of the Mighty One. Afterward, when a decree was made that if for thirty days any one should ask a petition of God or man, save of the king, he should be cast into a den of lions, Daniel, with firm, undaunted step, made his way to his chamber, and with his windows open prayed aloud three times a day, as he had done before. He was cast into the lions' den; but God sent holy angels to guard His servant (Signs of the Times, Aug. 14, 1884, par. 6).

He carried out his faith and principles against great opposition. He was condemned to death because he would not abate one jot of his allegiance to God even in the face of the king's decree. ...Daniel would allow no earthly power to come in between him and his God, even with the prospect of death in the den of lions (5T 527.1).

Through the moral courage of this one man who chose, even in the face of death, to take a right course rather than a politic one, Satan was defeated, and God honored. For the deliverance of Daniel from the power of the lions was a striking evidence that the Being whom he worshiped was the true and living God. And the king wrote unto "all people, nations, and languages, that dwell in all the earth:" "I make a decree, That in every dominion of my kingdom men tremble and fear before the God of Daniel; for He is the living God, and steadfast forever, and His kingdom that which shall not be destroyed, and His dominion shall be even unto the end" (Signs of the Times, November 4, 1886, paragraph 7).

Because of Daniel's faithfulness, King Darius recognized God as the only true God in the unchangeable law of the Medo-Persians. "The deliverance of Daniel from the den of lions had been used of God to create a favorable impression upon the mind of Cyrus the Great" (Prophets and Kings, p. 557 par. 1). Thus, when it was time for God's Jerusalem Temple to be rebuilt, King Cyrus issued the unchangeable decree to begin the restoration. But as Satan attempted to turn Daniel's faithfulness to God into his destruction in the early days of the Medo-Persian Empire, Satan also deceived King Ahasuerus to kill God's faithful people. And God warns us that Satan will try to do it again.

The decree that will finally go forth against the remnant people of God will be very similar to that issued by Ahasuerus against the Jews. Today the enemies of the true church see in the little company keeping the

Sabbath commandment, a Mordecai at the gate. The reverence of God's people for His law is a constant rebuke to those who have cast off the fear of the Lord and are trampling on His Sabbath (Prophets and Kings, p. 605.2).

Satan will arouse indignation against the minority who refuse to accept popular customs and traditions. Men of position and reputation will join with the lawless and the vile to take counsel against the people of God. Wealth, genius, education, will combine to cover them with contempt. Persecuting rulers, ministers, and church members will conspire against them. With voice and pen, by boasts, threats, and ridicule, they will seek to overthrow their faith. By false representations and angry appeals, men will stir up the passions of the people. Not having a "Thus saith the Scriptures" to bring against the advocates of the Bible Sabbath, they will resort to oppressive enactments to supply the lack. To secure popularity and patronage, legislators will yield to the demand for Sunday laws. But those who fear God, cannot accept an institution that violates a precept of the Decalogue. On this battlefield will be fought the last great conflict in the controversy between truth and error. And we are not left in doubt as to the issue. Today, as in the days of Esther and Mordecai, the Lord will vindicate His truth and His people (Prophets and Kings, p. 605.3).

Because Jerusalem's Temple had been indispensable to the Plan of Salvation, even though it was not in existence when the Persian Empire arose, when Daniel prayed three times a day, he faced toward where it had stood. The Sanctuary Services had involved worship, sinners offered sacrifices to atone for their sins, the priests daily offered morning and evening sacrifices, and the High Priest cleansed the Sanctuary yearly, i.e., to symbolize that God had accepted the repentance of His people and that He had forgiven their sins and removed the records of those sins. Its destruction was a big deal! King David expressed the importance of the Sanctuary in Psalms:

> The LORD hear thee in the day of trouble; the name of the God of Jacob defend thee; Send thee help from the Sanctuary (Psalms 20:1-2).

How could God's people be forgiven without a Temple and its Sanctuary Services? When Solomon dedicated the Temple, his prayer gave some insight into its importance:

> O LORD my God...That Thine eyes may be open toward this house night and day, [even] toward the place of which Thou hast said, My name shall be there: that Thou mayest *hearken unto the prayer which Thy servant shall make toward this place.* And <u>hearken Thou to the supplication of Thy servant, and of Thy people Israel, when they shall pray toward this place</u>: and hear Thou in heaven Thy dwelling place: and when Thou hearest, forgive... When Thy people Israel be smitten down before the enemy, because they have sinned against Thee, and shall turn again to Thee, and confess Thy name, and pray, and make supplication unto Thee in this house: Then hear thou in heaven, and forgive the sin of Thy people Israel, and bring them again unto the land which Thou gavest unto their fathers (1 Kings 8:28-30, 33-34).

The book that was sealed is...that portion of the prophecy of Daniel relating to the last days (Acts of the Apostles, page 585 paragraph 1).

Daniel was written in three *portions*: 1. Daniel 1:1-2:3 was in Hebrew—it explains how Daniel got to be in Babylon; 2. the so-called *historical* portion from Nebuchadnezzar's first dream to King Cyrus' reign (Daniel 2:4 to 7:28) was written in Aramaic; and 3. the third portion (Daniel 8:1-12:13) was written in Hebrew (see William H. Shea, *The Abundant Life Bible Amplifier*, pp. 20-21). Daniel's bilingual writing style is significant because some Aramaic (A) and Hebrew (H) words are the same, but their meanings are not always the same.

When Daniel 7 moves to chapter 8, Daniel switches from Aramaic to Hebrew. An English rendition of the Aramaic text in 7:2 is: "Four winds of the heaven strove upon the great sea." Look at Daniel's Aramaic words from the vantage point of the Hebrew meanings: "Four winds of heaven *guach* [(A) *strove*, (H) *brought forth*] *rab* [(A&H) *captains*] *yam* [(A) *great sea*, (H) *from the west*]." Comparing the Hebrew rendition of the Aramaic text in 7:2 "Four *living captains* came up *from out of the west*" to Daniel 7:17 "Four kings shall arise out of the earth." In that comparison, Daniel's vision and Heaven's interpretation are remarkably similar (4 captains = 4 kings).

Heaven's interpretation was sealed until the end time. No matter how precisely the translators translated the prophecies before they were unsealed, they could not explain the meanings that God had sealed until God ordained that they should be opened and understood.

"*The books of Daniel and the Revelation are one...but no further light was to be revealed before these messages had done their specific work*" (1MR 99.3). Daniel expands and explains his earlier visions in later visions that he sees by the "Ulai and Hiddekel Rivers" (Tigris and Euphrates). These visions are "now in process of fulfillment, and *ALL the events foretold will soon come to pass*" (16MR 334.2).

In this book are depicted scenes that are now in the past, and some... that are taking place around us; *other of its prophecies will not receive their complete fulfillment until the close of time* (RH, August 31, 1897, par. 5).

The people were not yet ready to meet their Lord. There was still a work of preparation to be accomplished for them. Light was to be given, directing their minds to the temple of God in Heaven; and as they should by faith follow their High Priest in His ministration there, new duties would be revealed. *Another message of warning and instruction was to be given to the church* (Great Controversy 1888, page 424 paragraph 3).

Light comes from the very throne of God. When some familiar truth presents itself to your mind in a new aspect, when a text of Scripture suddenly bursts upon you with new meaning like a flash of light that scatters the mist, and you see the relation of other truths to some part of the plan of redemption, God is leading you, and a divine Teacher is at your side. Will you not then open the door of your heart to receive more and more of the heavenly illumination? (Signs of the Times, Aug. 27, 1894, par. 3).

Heretofore those who presented the truths of the third angel's message have often been regarded as mere alarmists. Their predictions...have been pronounced groundless and absurd... But as...the event so long doubted and disbelieved is seen to be approaching, and the third message will produce an effect which it could not have had before (Great Controversy, p. 605 par. 3).

As we have followed down the chain of prophecy, revealed truth for our time has been clearly seen and explained. We are accountable for the privileges that we enjoy and for the light that shines upon our pathway. Those who lived in past generations were accountable for the light which was permitted to shine upon them. Their minds were exercised in regard to different points of Scripture which tested them. *But they did not understand the truths which we do. They were not responsible for the light which they did not have. They had the Bible, as we have; but the time for the unfolding of special truth in relation to the closing scenes of this earth's history is during the last generations that shall live upon the earth* (Testimonies Volume 2, p. 692 par. 2).

In the Scriptures are presented truths that relate especially to our own time. To the period just prior to the appearing of the Son of man, the prophecies of Scripture point, and here their warnings and threatenings preeminently apply. The prophetic periods of Daniel, extending to the very eve of the great consummation, throw a flood of light upon events then to transpire. The book of Revelation is also replete with warning and instruction for the last generation. The beloved John, under the inspiration of the Holy Spirit, portrays the fearful and thrilling scenes connected with the close of earth's history, and presents the duties and dangers of God's people. None need remain in ignorance, none need be unprepared for the coming of the day of God (Review and Herald, September 25, 1883, par. 6).

Those who have been in any measure blinded by the enemy, and who have not fully recovered themselves from the snare of Satan, will be in peril because they cannot discern light from heaven, and will be inclined to accept a falsehood. This will affect the whole tenor of their thoughts, their decisions, their propositions, their counsels. The evidences that God has given are no evidence to them, because they have blinded their own eyes by choosing darkness rather than light. Then they will originate something they call light, which the Lord calls sparks of their own kindling, by which they will direct their steps. The Lord declares, "Who is among you that feareth the Lord, that obeyeth the voice of His servant, that walketh in darkness, and hath no light? Let him trust in the name of the Lord, and stay upon his God. Behold, all ye that kindle a fire, that compass yourselves about with sparks: walk in the light of your fire, and in the sparks that ye have kindled. This shall ye have at Mine hand; ye shall lie down in sorrow." Jesus said, "For judgment I am come into this world, that they which see not might see; and that they which see might be made blind." "I am come a light into the world, that whosoever believeth on Me should not abide in darkness." "He that rejecteth Me, and receiveth not My words, hath one that judgeth him: the word that I have spoken, the same shall judge him in the last day" (SDA Bible Commentary Vol. 4, p. 1146 par. 10).

Such subjects as the sanctuary, in connection with the 2300 days, the commandments of God and the faith of Jesus, are perfectly calculated to explain the past Advent movement and show what our present position is, establish the faith of the doubting, and give certainty to the glorious future. These, I have frequently seen, were the principal subjects on which the messengers should dwell (Early Writings, page 63 paragraph 2).

It is possible to be a formal, partial believer, and yet be found wanting, and lose eternal life. It is possible to practice some of the Bible injunctions, and be regarded as a Christian, and yet perish because you are lacking in essential qualifications that constitute Christian character. The destroying angels have the commission from the Lord, "<u>Begin at My sanctuary</u>." And "they began at the ancient men which were before the house." If the warnings which God has given are neglected or regarded with indifference, if you suffer sin to be cherished, you are sealing your soul's destiny; you will be weighed in the balances and found wanting. Grace, peace, and pardon will be withdrawn forever; Jesus will have passed by, never again to come within the reach of your prayers and entreaties. While mercy still lingers, while Jesus is making intercession for us, let us make thorough work for eternity (Review and Herald, Jan. 11, 1887, par. 24).

By prayer man is braced for duty and prepared for trial. Morning and evening our earnest prayers should ascend to God...and is as acceptable to God as if offered in the sanctuary (ST, January 29, 1902, par. 2).

Daniel's Vision

People who disagree with a prophetic warning may justify their skepticism by claiming that the prophecy in question is being skewed by a private interpretation. But it may also be an attempt to protect cherished traditional beliefs. The word *idios* that is translated as *private* in 2 Peter 1:19-21 is also the root for the word *idiotic*. *True interpretations are not private or idiotic!* "Let us prophesy according to the proportion of faith" (Romans 12:6). "If all prophesy, and there come in one that believeth not, or one unlearned, he is convinced" (1 Corinthians 1:24).

It is not enough to have an intellectual knowledge of the truth. This alone cannot give the light and understanding essential to salvation. *There must be an entrance of the word into the heart. It must be set home by the power of the Holy Spirit.* The will must be brought into harmony with Its requirements. Not only the intellect but the heart and conscience must concur in the acceptance of the truth (RH, Sept 25, 1883, par. 7).

[God] employed pictures and symbols to represent to His prophets lessons which He would have them give to the people...through the sense of sight. Prophetic history was presented to Daniel and John in symbols...that he who read[s] might understand (1BC 1106.1).

Daniel 7 is true. It begins with a winged-lion, a fierce bear with three ribs in its mouth, a four-headed four-winged leopard, and an indescribable beast with iron teeth and brass claws. The Bible explains itself. "Winds...strove upon the great sea" (Daniel 7:2). "Thus, saith the LORD; Behold, I will raise up against Babylon, and against them that dwell in the midst of them that rise up against Me, a destroying wind" (Jeremiah 51:1). The gathered waters are *seas* (cf Genesis 1:10). "The *great sea* over against Lebanon" (Joshua 9:1) is the Mediterranean. Waters depict "peoples, and multitudes, and nations and tongues" (Revelation 17:15). "The great kingdoms that have ruled the world obtained their dominion by conquest and revolution, and they were presented to the prophet Daniel as beasts of prey, rising when the 'four winds of the heaven strove upon the great sea'" (Spirit of Prophecy Vol. 4, p. 276 par. 2). These beasts that arose from the sea depict kingdoms that ruled the area by the Mediterranean: Babylon, Medo-Persia, Greece, and Rome. Now that Daniel is unsealed, the historical understanding must not skew the final meaning that prepares us for Christ's Second Advent.

The visions of my head troubled me. I came near unto one of them that stood by, and asked him the truth of all this. So, he told me, and made me know the interpretation of the things. <u>These great beasts, which are four, *are* four kings, *which* shall arise out of the earth</u> (Daniel 7:15-17).

Heaven's spokesman did not focus on the four sea-beasts (kingdoms) that began chapter 7. Heaven gave the end time meaning: *These great beasts...[are] four kings, [which] shall arise out of the earth*. Heaven's true interpretation focused on *earth-kings* unlike the translators' rendition of Daniel 2 that replaced the kings with four kingdoms. As the translators ignored the king in Daniel 2, they ignored the kings in Heaven's clear interpretation of the *four beasts* in Daniel 7. After Heavens interpretation of the vision was disregarded, the kingdoms from Babylon to Rome that sealed the truth of the vision, concealed the end time truth.

The prophecies present a succession of events leading down to the opening of the Judgment. This is especially true of the book of Daniel. But that part of his prophecy which related to the last days, Daniel was bidden to close up and seal "to the time of the end." <u>Not till we reach this time could a message concerning the Judgment be proclaimed, based on a fulfillment of these prophecies.</u>

But at the time of the end, says the prophet, "many shall run to and fro, and knowledge shall be increased." [Daniel 12:4] (Great Controversy 1888, page 355 paragraph 3).

Those who will not accept the light in regard to the law of God will not understand the proclamation of the first, second, and third angel's messages. *The book of Daniel is unsealed in the revelation to John,* and carries us forward to the last scenes of this earth's history (Testimony to Ministers, page 115 paragraph 3).

When Revelation 13:5 unseals Daniel 7:25, it deals with the same period of time. "And now began the 1260 years [538-1798] of papal oppression foretold in the prophecies of Daniel and John. [Daniel 7:25; Revelation 13:5-7]" (Spirit of Prophecy Vol. 4, p. 57.2). And the second beast in Revelation 13:11-18 is identified as the power from the *prophetic earth* that has the ability to call fire down from heaven:

I beheld another beast coming up out of the earth; and he had *duo* horns like a lamb, and he spoke as a dragon. And he exercised all the power of the first beast before him, and caused the earth and them which dwell therein to worship the first beast, whose deadly wound was healed. And he doeth great wonders, so that <u>he maketh fire come down from heaven on the earth in the sight of men</u> (Revelation 13:11-13, supplemented).

[Beware lest we should] mangle the visions, spiritualize away their literal meaning, and throw a satanic influence upon...[them] and call it the power of God (cf Spiritual Gifts Vol. 2, page 73 paragraph 1).

Hiroshima and Nagasaki confirm America's identity as the *earth-beast* of Revelation 13. The USA is the only country that has literally rained fire down from the sky. As prophetic fulfilment continues, President Trump has threatened to rain "FIRE AND FURY" on North Korea (August 2017).

Over the city of Hiroshima, the *Enola Gay* dropped an ...atomic weapon... *Two thousand feet above the ground, the bomb...detonated* (www.Factmonster.com).

After the flash, she [West] saw a brilliant orange orb...*erupt in the sky*... the buildings around her and much of the city were on fire... (www.nydailynews.com).

Over Nagasaki...the Fat Man was *exploded above the ground* (www.en.Wikipedia.org).

Vice President Pence has stated, "The time has come to establish the United States Space Force" (www.washington post.com). "The U.S. Space Command officially starts Aug. 29, [2019] serving as the launching pad for the Space Force, they said. Air Force Gen. John Raymond has been... confirmed by the Senate as its first leader" (www.msn.com).

Revelation 13's *earth-beast* is the USA; the kings from the *earth* in Daniel 7 are American Presidents! The Bible says: "Put the crown upon him...they made him king" (2 Kings 11:12). "He shall be king...I have appointed him to be ruler" (1 Kings 1:35). White reaffirms: "The crown removed from Israel passed successively to the kingdoms of Babylon, Medo-Persia, Greece, and Rome" (Education, p. 179). "Crowned heads, presidents, rulers in high places" (RH, August 17, 1897, par. 14). The sea-beasts of Daniel 7:1-3 foreshadows end time US Presidents. When Heaven's interpretation is applied to the vision in Daniel 7, their identity is revealed.

Before the Judgment in Heaven convened, Daniel saw the thrones from Babylon to the ten tribes that divided the Imperial Roman Empire *cast down* and new thrones set up or *placed* by the succeeding kings and kingdoms. The Catholic Bible translates the phrase *thrones cast down* (KJV) as *thrones were placed* (Daniel 7:9, Douay-Rheims). Thus, Daniel's vision is also describing the Judgment scene that occurs in Heaven after thrones were both *cast down* and *put in place*. The usage of terms with dual meanings in Daniel 7 is prophetically significant. Daniel describes events that he saw happening on earth prior to and after 1844 as well as events that he was seeing in Heaven relating to the 1844 Judgment. Daniel is not making statements that *must be read as either this or that*, but *he is saying both this and that* (both *cast down* and *placed*; both *on earth* and *in Heaven*). Satan's throne has been cast down from Heaven. "How art thou fallen *from heaven*, O Lucifer... How art thou *cut down...* For thou hast said in thine heart, I will ascend into heaven, *I will exalt my throne above the stars* [angels] of God...I will ascend above the heights of the clouds [angels]; I will be like the Highest" (Isaiah 14:12-14, margin). Conversely, "The LORD'S throne is in heaven" (Psalms 11:4). And thrones are placed or set up for "I saw thrones, and they sat upon them, and judgment was given unto them" (Revelation 20:4).

Christ had come, not to the earth, as they [Millerite Adventists] expected [in 1844], but, as foreshadowed in the type, to the most holy place of the temple of God in Heaven. He is represented by the prophet Daniel as coming at this time to the Ancient of days: "I saw in the night visions, and, behold, one like the Son of man came with the clouds of heaven, and came"—not to the earth, but— "to the Ancient of days, and they brought Him near before Him [Daniel 7:13]" (GC88, p. 424 par. 1).

This coming is foretold also by the prophet Malachi. "The Lord, whom ye seek, shall suddenly come to His temple, even the messenger of the covenant, whom ye delight in: behold, He shall come, saith the Lord of hosts." [Malachi 3:1.] The coming of the Lord to His temple [in 1844] was sudden, unexpected, to His people. They were not looking for Him there. They expected Him to come to earth, "in flaming fire taking vengeance on them that know not God, and that obey not the gospel" [2 Thessalonians 1:8] (Great Controversy 1888, p. 424.2).

The Adventists, who awaited Christ's return in 1844 had the wrong event. They entirely misunderstood Christ's going to Heaven's Temple to stand for His people, the Investigative Judgment. But the event was only wrong because of the timing. When Christ finishes the judgment in Heaven and declares, "It is done!" *He will come in vengeance, as they had anticipated in 1843 & 44, in fulfillment of the same prophecy!*

Those faithful...ones, who could not understand why their Lord did not come, were not left in darkness. Again, they were led to their Bibles to search the prophetic periods... *They saw that the prophetic periods reached to 1844, and that the same evidence they had presented to show that the prophetic periods closed in 1843, proved that they would terminate in 1844.* Light from the word of God shone upon their position, and they discovered a tarrying time. --If the vision tarry, wait for it. --In their love for Jesus' immediate coming, they had overlooked the tarrying of the vision, which was calculated to manifest the true waiting ones (1SG 138.1).

The *same evidence* that proved that the 2300 years ended in 1843 proved that they ended again in 1844! Likewise, the same evidence in the prophecy of Daniel 7 will prove that Christ will Come after the judgment ends! Though we do not know the day or the hour, God's word is preparing us.

Read the book of Daniel. Call up, point by point, the history of the kingdoms there represented. *Behold statesmen,* councils, powerful armies, and see how God wrought to abase the pride of men, and lay human glory in the dust. God alone is represented as great. *In the vision of the prophet, He is seen casting down one mighty ruler, and setting up another* (4BC 1166.4).

In Daniel 7, the vision is sequential thru the Judgment Hour, which is followed by the destruction of the 4th beast. *"The Judgment was set, and the books were opened."* After the 1844 Judgement, Daniel hears "the voice of the great words which the horn spake" (Daniel 7:10, 11). Pope John-

Paul II spoke great things in his Apostolic Letter, Dies Domini (the Lord's Day), a teaching of peace, in which he accused God of lying. Dies Domini asserts that the God, who does not change, changed Sabbath to Sunday. Issued May 31, 1998, the 6th of Sivan, which according to Jewish Tradition, "On the 6th Sivan...after the Exodus, G-d revealed Himself on Mount Sinai" and God gave the Ten Commandments (cf www. Chabad.org). Do not miss this: On the anniversary of the day that God said, "Remember the Sabbath Day, to keep it holy" (Exodus 20:8), Pope John-Paul II nullified God's Sabbath Commandment. Daniel "beheld [even] till the beast was slain, and his body destroyed, and given to the burning flame." The 4th beast, an *earth-king*, President, who heard the post1844 Pope John-Paul II speak, is consumed by the flames at Christ's Advent that the Adventists had anticipated in 1844.

"As concerning the rest of the beasts," three Presidents depicted by the lion, bear, and leopardlike beasts: "They had their dominion taken away: yet their lives were prolonged for a season and time" (Daniel 7:12, 11). There are 4 seasons in a year: 90 days is 1/4th of a 360-day prophetic year. Since the *season and time* relate to men, the 90 days depict 90 years, but the *time* is not 360 years since men do not live that long. The prophecy is identifying the *season and time*, the 91 years, preceding the 4th beast's destruction. *This is the end time meaning that has been sealed that is needed now.*

President Reagan turned 90 years old on February 6, 2001. In his 91st year, the 9/11/01 tragedy struck America. It aligns with the prophetic *season and time* of 7:12, in which Reagan, Bush I, and Clinton had *had their dominion taken away: yet their lives were prolonged.* Thus, the American Presidents that are depicted as sea-beasts *like a lion, that had eagle's wings; a bear, raised up on one side, with three ribs in the mouth; and a leopard, which had upon the back of it four wings of a fowl; the beast had also four heads* (cf 7:4-6) are: Reagan, the Great Orator (a lion's mouth); Bush I, his wars to bring about a New World Order were depicted as the three ribs in his mouth, i.e., Panama, Somalia, and Iraq; and

Clinton, the leopardlike features. While he was embroiled in scandal, America's four Joint Chiefs of Staff managed hot spots. The leopard aligns with the idol's brass midsection in Daniel 2. His midsection almost got him put out of office.

The "ten horns that [were] in his head, and [of] the other which came up, and before whom three fell; even [of] that horn that had eyes, and a mouth that spake very great things, whose look [was] more stout than his fellows" (Daniel 7:20) links America to the papacy. The 10 Presidents bonding with the seven post-1929 popes were: Truman, Eisenhower, Kennedy, Johnson, Nixon, Ford, Carter, Reagan, Bush I, and Clinton. "Harry Truman was put in office by the Jesuits, the Pendergast Democratic machine in Missouri" (www.the forbiddenknowledge.com). Daniel's prophecy moved from the papacy in 1798 to America that annexed the *prophetic earth* in 1803; the home of Truman, who rained down fire. The next nine Presidents all had meetings with the popes.

The charismatic Pope John-Paul II plucked up: Reagan, Bush I, and Clinton. He bonded so thoroughly with them that the post-1929 papacy was depicted as a leopardlike beast (Revelation 13). In vision, John "saw one of his heads as it were wounded to death; and his deadly wound was healed: and all the world wondered after the beast" (Revelation 13:3). Like the papacy that had recovered from its 1798 wound, Pope John-Paul II recovered from an assassination attempt. By recognizing Pope John-Paul II, the head of the Catholic Church, as a head of state, Reagan continued Mussolini's healing of the papacy's deadly political wound on America's behalf. Bush I continued the papacy's religious healing, when he declared Pope John-Paul II to be the world's *moral leader,* i.e., *the head of all the churches*: "I had an opportunity to express my profound gratitude to the Holy Father for the *spiritual and moral leadership...*" (www.bush41library.tamu.edu). And President Clinton sang the praises of Pope John-Paul II: "Whether I agree or disagree with him, this guy is on my side" (www.nbcnews.com). *42 months after 9/11/01, Pope John-Paul II died, April 2, 2005.*

The Little Horn

Understand, O son of man: for <u>at the time of the end</u> <u>[shall be] the vision</u>... I will make thee know what shall be <u>in the last end of the indignation: for at the time</u> <u>appointed the end [shall be]</u>. The ram which thou sawest having *two* horns [pushing toward] the kings of Media and Persia (Daniel 8:17, 19, 20, margin).

Before Daniel's prophecies were fulfilled, I misconstrued some of them. Thus, I constantly go back to the Bible to harmonize my views with the Scriptures. I expected that the President following Clinton, would be the 666-image beast of Revelation 13: Albert [6] Arnold [6] Gore II [6]. "And his body destroyed, and given to the burning flame" (Daniel 7:11). I was wrong: George [6] Walker [6] Bush [4] became President Bush II, e.g., President George [6] Walker [6] Bush II [6]. [He pushed at Iraq, a part of ancient Media, and Christ did not come.] Instead, as the two empires, Imperial and Papal Rome, were depicted as one beast whose "teeth *were of* iron, and his nails *of* brass" (7:19), <u>Bush II and Obama became as</u> <u>though they were one</u>. [Obama pushed at Iran.] These Presidents align with Revelation 13's transition from the first sea-beast (the papacy) to the 2nd beast from the earth with the two horns. Thus, President Obama, the 2nd horn on the earth-beast, also had to be the man with the 666 of Bible prophecy. The <u>coincidental evidence</u> was substantial:

    1) When Barack Obama was announced the President elected from Illinois, "The numbers 6-6-6 were the winning combination in an Illinois lottery" (<u>www. snopes.com</u>).]

    2) Counting the *letters that double as numbers* in the pope's title, VICARIUS FILII DEI: I (1), V (5), [U is a form of V], L (50), C (100), and D (500). With non-Roman Numerals removed, the numbers are: [VI (6) + C (100) + IV (4)] = 110, [IL (49) + II (2)] = 51, [D (500) + I (1)] = 501, which total 663. But because VICARIUS FILII DEI is a title, the sequencing of the numbers does not follow the rules for Roman Numerals

where an I would never be placed before an L. So, when VICARIUS FILII DEI, is counted, the numerals must be listed in vertical columns with single digits. That eliminates the incorrect sequencing of IL. For consistency, it also changes the sequencing of IV that is 4 to a value of 6.

VICARIUS FILII DEI		
V= 5	I= 1	D=500
I= 1	L=50	I= 1
C=100	I= 1	
I= 1	I= 1	
U [V]= 5		
112	53	501 =666

The number (666) of the Image Beast was made up; [Revelation 13:18.] and that it was the Beast that changed the Sabbath, and the Image Beast had followed on after, and kept the Pope's, and not God's Sabbath. And all we were required to do, was to give up God's Sabbath, and keep the Pope's, and then we should have the mark of the Beast, and of his image (WLF 19.1).

For Revelation 13's *2nd-beast to be an image of the papal beast, it must also have the number 666.* After Pope Pius VI died in captivity, James Monroe was the US President linked to the prophetic-earth, i.e., the 1803 Louisiana Purchase. *The Monroe Doctrine spoke like a dragon;* warning the Europeans: *Stop colonizing the Americas or else!*

"The number of a *man*" is 666 (Revelation 13:18); the pope's title: VICARIUS FILII DEI is 666. Man (*anthropos*) also is *men*: "Fishers of *men* [*anthropos*]" (Matthew 4:19). The word *autos can be his or their:* "His [*autos*] number is 666" "all liars shall have *their* [*autos*] part in...the second death" (Revelation 13:18; 21:8). *The number of men, their number is 666* (13:18, alternate). Counting the *number of the letters* in the

Presidents' names from Monroe to Obama, the papal beast's number 666 is made up by the image-beast.

American Presidents	Letters
James Monroe	11
John Quincy Adams	15
Andrew Jackson	13
Martin Van Buren	14
William Henry Harrison	20
John Tyler II	11
James Knox Polk	13
Zachary Taylor	13
Millard Fillmore	15
Franklin Pierce	14
James Buchanan II	15
Abraham Lincoln	14
Andrew Johnson	13
Ulysses Simpson Grant	19
Rutherford Birchard Hayes	23
James Abram Garfield	18
Chester Alan Arthur	17
Stephen Grover Cleveland	22
Benjamin Harrison	16
William McKinley II	17
Theodore Roosevelt II	19
William Howard Taft	17
Woodrow Wilson	13
Warren Gamaliel Harding	21
Calvin Coolidge	14
Herbert Clark Hoover	18
Franklin Delano Roosevelt	23
Harry S Truman	12
Dwight David Eisenhower	21
John Fitzgerald Kennedy	21
Lyndon Baines Johnson	19
Richard Milhous Nixon	19
Gerald Rudolph Ford II	19

James Earl Carter II	17
Ronald Wilson Reagan	18
George Herbert Walker Bush	23
William Jefferson Clinton	23
George Walker Bush	16
Barack Hussein Obama II	20
Total letters in their] President's names	666

3) Coincidentally, Mr. Obama was also America's 44th President. Ancient Israel's 44th king was its last.

4) President Obama was elected in 2008. "The vision of the evening and the morning which was told [is] true: wherefore shut thou up the vision for it [shall be] for *many days*" (Daniel 8:26). The word *day[s]* is in the Bible 2008 times. A day can be a year: *The vision is true—shut up the vision; for it shall be [coincidently] for the year 2008?* Noah was a "preacher of righteousness" (2 Peter 2:5) for 120 years. The Seventh-day Adventist Church rejected Righteousness by Faith in Minneapolis in 1888. White "SPOKE TWENTY TIMES IN MINNEAPOLIS... SHE PLEADED FOR OPEN MINDED BIBLE STUDY. SHE HERSELF DID NOT SPEAK ON THE TOPIC OF RIGHTEOUSNESS BY FAITH." "A. T. JONES, SPEAKING OF THE RECEPTION OF THE TRUTHS SET FORTH AT MINNEAPOLIS, REPORTED: 'I KNOW THAT SOME THERE ACCEPTED IT; OTHERS REJECTED IT ENTIRELY'" (3SM 158.3 - 4). Like it was in Noe's Day and Israel's rejection of God's leading that caused their 40-year wilderness trek, did rejecting Righteousness by Faith in 1888 delay Christ's Advent: *Shut up the true vision until* 2008?

Reality requires me to reconcile my prophetic views with the facts. The prophecy has moved from the papal-beast to the USA. The two horns, i.e., rulers, has depicted Presidents Bush and Obama! The meaning of the word *two* in this text has to be examined. In Luke 10: 1, Jesus sent His disciples out *ana duo*: *By twos* (NASB) or *by two and two* (KJV). Though *duo* occurs once in this text, it is translated as *two and two*. Revelation 13 confirms that *duo* is *two and two!*

Then came President Trump, the 3rd horn on Revelation 13's earth-beast that Bible prophecy says is to have two lamblike horns. "*Two* horns *are* the kings" and "the great horn that *is* between his eyes *is* the...king" (Daniel 8:20, 21). Though the facts are correct, my Bible study reached a wrong conclusion. Was I presumptuous or did I view reality like Abraham, King Nebuchadnezzar, Miller, and others, whose prophetic insights got it wrong before the prophecies were fulfilled? While my critics focus on my errors, I pray and search the Bible for the true answers! What did I miss?

> We have nothing to fear for the future, except as we shall forget the way the Lord has led us, and His teaching in our past history (Life Sketches, p. 196 par. 2).

How did God lead His people in our past history? He allowed us to get things wrong before we got them right! He did not forsake us when we made honest errors. He led those, who are willing to follow, from error to a more correct understanding of Bible prophecy if we yielded our *views of reality* and accepted the increased knowledge that God sees fit to give to us at His appointed time. God does not always lead His people by giving us an infallible view of His word, but by faith we follow His word. Faith is not presumption:

> When the soul is filled with the Spirit of the Lord, sweet, heartfelt praise to God glorifies Him. Some have professed to have great faith in God, and to have special gifts and special answers to their prayers, although the evidence was lacking. <u>They mistook presumption for faith</u>. The prayer of faith is never lost; but to claim that it will be always answered in the very way and for the particular thing we have expected, is presumption (Testimony Vol. 1, page 231 paragraph 1).

As I have imparted the light given me. I have very much more light on the Old and New Testament

Scriptures, which I shall present to our people if my way is not blocked (Manuscript Release Vol. 9, p. 23 par. 2).

"There is nothing in the word of God to be thrown aside" (Signs of the Times, June 3, 1886, par. 13). "The Bible must be your counselor. Study it and the testimonies God has given; for they never contradict His Word" (3SM 32. 3).

Study Bible prophecy! The papal sea-beast's 7th head was Pope Benedict XVI; he yielded to the US (image-beast) with *duo horns* during the reign of Bush II (666). Obama was the 2nd horn on the earth-beast! The letters in the President's names from Monroe to Obama ended at 666. But he was not the last horn! Allegations of Russian meddling tainted (horn 3) Trump's election. Biden's election (horn 4) is tainted by voter fraud allegations. Kamala [6] Harris [6] Emhoff [6] is likely the closer, but though *duo horns on the earth-beast can be two and two; they are not five.* Thus, Biden and Harris likely rule jointly as if America has two end time Presidents.

At this point another symbol is introduced. Says the prophet, "I beheld *another beast coming up out of the earth*; and *he had two horns like a lamb.*" [Revelation 13:11.] Both the appearance of this beast and the manner of its rise indicate that *the nation which it represents is unlike those presented under the preceding symbols* (Great Controversy 1888, p. 440 par. 1).

As Daniel 4 had predicted that Nebuchadnezzar, the king of Babylon would recover from his deadly wound; the papacy received its deadly wound after it ruled for 42 months (1260 years from 538 to 1798). Mussolini healed that wound in 1929. Pope John-Paul II also received an assassination wound that almost killed him. From 9/11/2001, the *season and time* (Daniel 7:12), the 1260 days allotted to him ended February 22, 2005 when he no longer ruled the papacy, for he was dying. He made a video 2/22/2005 (cf USA Today), and was hospitalized the next day. Pope John-Paul II remained hospitalized, on life support, until he died.

On the Gregorian calendar, the prophecy was fulfilled when Pope John-Paul II died at the end of 42-full months. In September 2001 and April 2005, the days that exceed the 42full months confirm that *duo* also means *two and two*. Bible writers used the Hebrew calendar. To synchronize it with the solar calendar, "A leap year occurs 7 times in the 19-year Metonic cycle. With years 3, 6, 8, 11, 14, 17, and 19 of the cycle being leap years" (www.Timeanddate.com). Adar I, "The extra month is inserted before the regular month of Adar" (www.jewfaq.Org). In the phrase, "To continue *forty* [and] *two* months" (Revelation 13:5), the word for 40 is always 40 in the Bible, but *duo* is not always *two* in the Bible. From 9/11/01 to 4/2/05, Adar I was added exactly twice on the Hebrew calendar. Thus, Pope John-Paul II died *42 regular months* plus *two* months to the very day! This confirms that the *two and two* reading of *duo* in Luke 10:1 is the correct reading of the final fulfillment of the *40-duo* months and the *duo horns* in Revelation 13.

> The dragon gave him his power, and his seat, and great authority. And I saw one of his heads as it were wounded to death; and his deadly wound was healed: and all the world wondered after the beast. And they worshipped the dragon which gave power unto the beast: and they worshipped the beast, saying, Who [is] like unto the beast? Who is able to make war with him? And there was given unto him a mouth speaking great things and blasphemies; and <u>power was given unto him to continue forty and two months</u>... [Revelation 13:4-10, quoted.] *<u>This entire chapter is a revelation of what will surely take place</u>* (SDA Bible Commentary Vol. 7, p. 979 par. 10).

The end time 42-month time prophecy will surely take place: "<u>In the last days...will take place the final fulfillment of the Revelator's prophecy. [13:4-18, quoted.]</u>" (19MR 282.1). White's prophetic repetition of the 42 months was verified:

The reference you asked about is correct. ...So, it does indeed refer to these verses in Revelation 13, and this is the prophecy that she mentioned just before the reference. ...I confirmed it by going to the manuscript, where the verses were written out (William Fagal, Associate Director, Ellen G. White Estate, 12501 Old Columbia Pike, Silver Spring, MD 20904-6600 U.S.A).

The world wondered after Pope John-Paul II. Who could make war with him? "Communism fell as a result of the activities of the Apostolic See and John-Paul II" (www. miszlivetzferenc.com). Who resisted his charisma? It awed Reagan, Bush I, and Clinton. But though John-Paul II was the little horn in Daniel 7, he is not the horn in chapter 8.

Daniel 8 resumes with Presidents Bush II and Obama, the end time horns on the ram that moves across the land/earth, America. The horn that is to be broken on the goat is Trump. I expected him to be removed from office by an unusual event rather than an election, and Michael Pence would have been the little horn of Daniel 8. IT DID NOT HAPPEN! Joe Biden was President March 29, 2021. He is the last of the *two and two lamblike horns* on the earth-beast in Revelation 13, and the Little Horn of Daniel 8 that wages war against Christ and His people! By Babylonian custom, if Kamala [6] Harris [6] (Emhoff [6]) should be President after March 29, Christ would come before the next March 29 because there are not 5 horns. Love your Savior, Jesus! Watch Bible prophecy and current events!

The scriptures are very clear: "If the watchman see the sword come, and blow not the trumpet, and the people be not warned; if the sword come, and take *any* person from among them, he is taken away in his iniquity; but his blood will I require at the watchman's hand" (Ezekiel 33:6). As a Bible student, I have been under conviction to share what I know to the best of my understanding. You must study for yourself to be in God's presence, a worker that will not be ashamed.

Daniel Repeats

The burden of Christ's preaching was, "The time is fulfilled, and the kingdom of God is at hand; repent ye, and believe the gospel." Thus, *the gospel message, as given by the Saviour Himself, was based on the prophecies.* The "time" which He declared to be fulfilled was the period made known by the angel Gabriel to Daniel. "Seventy weeks," said the angel, "are determined upon thy people and upon thy holy city, to finish the transgression, and to make an end of sins, and to make reconciliation for iniquity, and to bring in everlasting righteousness, and to seal up the vision and prophecy, and to anoint the most holy." Daniel 9:24. A day in prophecy stands for a year. See Numbers 14:34; Ezekiel 4:6. The seventy weeks, or four hundred and ninety days, represent four hundred and ninety years. A starting point for this period is given: "Know therefore and understand, that from the going forth of the commandment to restore and to build Jerusalem unto the Messiah the Prince shall be seven weeks, and threescore and two weeks," sixty-nine weeks, or four hundred and eighty-three years. Daniel 9:25. The commandment to restore and build Jerusalem, as completed by the decree of Artaxerxes Longimanus (see Ezra 6:14; 7:1, 9, margin), went into effect in the autumn of B. C. 457. From this time four hundred and eighty-three years extend to the autumn of A. D. 27. According to the prophecy, this period was to reach to the Messiah, the Anointed One. In A. D. 27, Jesus at His baptism received the anointing of the Holy Spirit, and soon afterward began His ministry. Then the message was proclaimed. "The time is fulfilled" (DA 233.1).

Then, said the angel, "He shall confirm the covenant with many for one week [seven years]." For seven years after the Saviour entered on His ministry, the gospel was to be preached especially to the Jews; for three and a half years by Christ Himself; and afterward by the apostles. "In the midst of the week He shall cause the sacrifice and the oblation to cease." Daniel 9:27. In the spring of A. D. 31, Christ the true sacrifice was offered on Calvary. Then the veil of the temple was rent in twain, showing that the sacredness and significance of the sacrificial service had departed. <u>The time had come for the earthly sacrifice and oblation to cease</u> (DA 233.2).

The one week--seven years--ended in A. D. 34. Then by the stoning of Stephen the Jews finally sealed their rejection of the gospel... (DA 233.3).

<u>The time</u> of Christ's coming, His anointing by the Holy Spirit, His death, and the giving of the gospel to the Gentiles, were <u>definitely pointed out</u>. It was the privilege of the Jewish people to understand these prophecies, and to recognize their fulfillment in the mission of Jesus. Christ urged upon His disciples *the importance of prophetic study.* Referring to the prophecy given to Daniel in regard to their time, He said, "Whoso readeth, *let him understand.*" Matthew 24:15... (Desire of Ages, p. 234.1).

Not at first had God revealed the exact time of the first advent; and even when the prophecy of Daniel made this known, not all rightly interpreted the message (PK 700.1).

These prophecies had been literally fulfilled in Jesus of Nazareth...the sure word of prophecy (AA 124.3).

As the message of Christ's First Advent announced the kingdom of His grace, so the message of His Second Advent announces the kingdom of His glory. And <u>*the second message, like the first, is based on the prophecies.*</u> *The words of the angel to Daniel relating to the last days were to be understood in the time of the end* (DA 234.4).

The time has come for Daniel to stand in his lot. The time has come for the light given him to go to the world *as never before.* If those for whom the Lord has done so much will walk in the light, *their <u>knowledge of Christ and the prophecies relating to Him will be greatly increased as they near the close of this earth's history</u>* (21MR 407.3).

The message of Christ's First Advent was based on the prophecies in Daniel 9 and 11. *The message of Christ's Second Advent is based on these same prophecies repeated.*

The truth for this time, the third angel's message, is to be proclaimed with a loud voice, meaning with increasing power, as we approach the great final test... The present truth for this time comprises the messages, the third angel's message succeeding the first and the second. The presentation of this message with all it embraces is our work. We stand as the remnant people in <u>these last days to promulgate the truth and swell the cry of the third angel's wonderful distinct message</u>, giving the trumpet a certain sound. Eternal truth, which we have adhered to from the beginning, is to be maintained in all its increasing importance to the close of probation. *The trumpet is to give no uncertain sound* (9MR 291.1).

...At the end of the days. John sees the little book unsealed. Then *Daniel's prophecies have their proper place in the first, second, and third angels' messages* to be given to the world. *<u>The unsealing of the little book was the message in relation to time</u>* (1MR 99.2).

Based on the prophecies in Daniel 9 that Gabriel revealed to Daniel: "Seventy weeks are determined upon thy people..." (Daniel 9:24). In the end time, they are not 490 prophetic years: "Know therefore and understand, that from the going forth of the commandment to restore and to build Jerusalem unto the messiah, the prince, shall be seven weeks, and threescore and two weeks" (9:25). Gabriel's words have more than one meaning. The alternate end time meanings repeat and enlarge the prophecy to the anointed one.

> *Know therefore and understand that from the going forth of the command to apostatize by the mother to the children teaching peace unto the anointing of the ruler shall be seven weeks and threescore and two weeks. This is enlarged: from the mother's decree to the children, the time of anguish shall come again* (Daniel 9:25, alternate).

Jerusalem means *Teaching of Peace.* The Roman mother church's end time command to restore and build Jerusalem, her decree *teaching peace, Dies Domini* (May 31, 1998), links Sunday to *peace* in sections 1, 18, 26, 33, 44, 52, 67, & 73. In the end time, Daniel 9:25 means: From the going forth of the May 31, 1998 *command to apostatize,* to the anointing of the *ruler* is 69 weeks. *This time of anguish shall come again.* [The 69 weeks double to 138 weeks.] From the *command to apostatize* issued Sunday, May 31, 1998, the 138 weeks ended on Saturday, January 20, 2001. It was the very day that America's Protestant counterfeit prince of the covenant, George Walker Bush, was anointed as President of the USA! The end time message of Daniel 9 has begun to proclaim: "The time is fulfilled!" Prophecy has met end time history.

> And after threescore and two weeks shall messiah be cut off, but not for himself: and the people of the prince that shall come shall destroy the city and the sanctuary; and the end thereof [shall be] with a flood, and unto the end of the war desolations are determined (Daniel 9:26).

Threescore, initially translated as *six* multiplied by *ten,* in *certain* instances, it is the number added to *ten* (cf Strong's). The fulfillment of 9:26 confirms that *sixteen* is the correct end time reading. The word following *sixteen* is *two,* which is *twice* or *double* (cf Nehemiah 23:20 & 2 Kings 2:9; 6:10). Sixteen weeks doubled are 32 weeks. *Cut off* also means to *fail.* The end time meaning: *After 32 weeks, the anointed*

Protestant prince fails (Daniel 9:26). Bush II failed September 1, 2001, exactly 32 weeks *after* being anointed the Prince of America's Constitution, President Bush II failed to keep the US safe. A surprise attack changed everything forever.

> *After thirty-two weeks,* the anointed one [Bush II] shall fail. The prince's people shall attack and destroy the city's set apart places to cut them asunder. At the end of time, he will become incensed with anger even unto the end of the war that is appalling and decisive (Daniel 9:26, end time alternate reading, supplemented).

A *sanctuary* is a *set apart place, a treasure house.* One *Twin Tower* was a set apart *treasure house* with a vault of gold. *Satan is the prince of this world. His men destroyed it.*

> And *he shall confirm the constitution with many for one week: and in the midst of the week, he shall cause the sacrifice and the oblation to cease,* and for the overspreading of abominations he shall make [it] desolate, even until the consummation, and that determined shall be poured upon the desolate (9:27).

> I, George W. Bush, President of the United States ... hereby proclaim...September 17 through September 23, 2001, as Constitution Week (www.presidency.ucsb.edu).

In the midst of *Constitution Week* (Sept. 17 to 23, 2001), Thursday (9/20/01), America's apostate Protestant prince of the covenant caused Christ's *Sacrifice* and *Oblation to cease.* President George W. Bush stated the following:

> I also want to speak tonight directly to Muslims throughout the world. We respect your faith... *Its teachings are good* and peaceful, and those who commit evil in the name of Allah blaspheme the name of Allah (www.americanrhetoric.com).

A popular view today is that Christians, Muslims, and Jews worship the same God. But Muslims reject Jesus as the Son of God and the Jews cursed themselves: "His [Christ's] blood [be] on us, and on our children" (Matthew 27:22-25). Salvation without Christ is a heathen notion that voids Christ's Sacrifice and Oblation.

The idea that it is necessary only to develop the good that exists in man by nature, is a fatal deception. "The natural man receiveth not the things of the Spirit of God: for they are foolishness unto him: neither can he know them, because they are spiritually discerned." ...1 Corinthians 2:14; 3:7. Of Christ, it is written...the only "name under heaven given among men, whereby we must be saved" John 1:4; Acts 4:12 (SC 18.2).

Christ's *Sacrifice* on Calvary was to save us from eternal death. The *Oblation* is the necessity for us to receive Jesus as our *personal Savior*. Christ's death is useless in our behalf unless we accept Him as the Atonement for our sins. Bush II's speech did away with Jesus as our personal Savior.

The prosperity of the soul depends upon Christ's atoning sacrifice. He came to this world to obtain forgiveness in our behalf. *Our first work is to strive most earnestly for spiritual blessings, in order that we may be kept loyal and true amidst the perils of these last days kept from yielding one inch to Satan's devices.* It is the duty of every one to make straight paths for his feet, lest the lame be turned out of the way. We have no time to lose. The prosperity of the soul depends upon the oneness that Christ prayed might exist among those who believe in Him. They are to be one with Him as He is One with the Father. Drawing apart from one another is not God's plan, but the plan of the artful foe (TDG 74.3).

We are to beware of those who...would if possible, deceive the very elect... Those who are departing from the faith are at work to undermine the confidence of others... Our warnings come from the One who...sees our dangers, and is acquainted with the conniving of those who are opposed to His truth... He who is our Intercessor in the heavenly courts will purify His people (TDG 74.4 – 5).

The *Ten Days of Awe* precede Yom Kippur, the Day of Atonement. In ancient Israel, each day of awe was set aside to review one of the Ten Commandments to make sincere confession to God in preparation for Yom Kippur, which was September 27, 2001. On the 3rd Day of Awe, when God's people would have been confessing their sins regarding the 3rd commandment: "Thou shalt not take the name of the LORD thy God in vain (Exodus 20:7), Christians, in name only, take God's name in vain! President Bush II took Christ's name in vain when he voided Christ's *Sacrifice* and *Oblation.*

Today this sacrilegious work is being more than repeated. There will be messages borne; and those who have rejected the messages God has sent, will hear most startling declarations. The Holy Spirit will invest the announcement with a sanctity and solemnity which will appear terrible in the ears of those who have heard the pleadings of infinite love, and have not responded to the offers of pardon and forgiveness. Injured and insulted Deity will speak, proclaiming the sins that have been hidden. As the priests and rulers, full of indignation and terror, sought refuge in flight at the last scene of the cleansing of the temple, *so will it be in the work for these last days. The woes that will be pronounced upon those that have had light from heaven, and yet did not heed it, they will feel, but will have no power to act.* This is represented in the parable of the wise and foolish virgins. They cannot obtain a character from the wise virgins, and they have no oil of grace to discern the clear light or to accept it. They cannot light their lamps and join the procession that goes in to the marriage supper of the Lamb (SpTA07 54.2).

The 490 literal weeks in Daniel 9 reveals were fulfilled *twice* in the end time: Seven 70-week periods during the Bush II Presidency, and a 2nd 70 weeks during Obama's. Understand the words and the vision [*mareh* (what is seen)]. Seventy weeks are determined 7 times upon thy people [Daniel 9:23-27]. Consider this overview:

1st 70...**to awaken and prepare the people**
Bush II: May 31, 1998 to October 2, 1999
Obama: Oct. 21, 2007 to February 21, 2009

2nd 70...**to finish known rebellion**
Bush II: October 3, 1999 to February 3, 2001
Obama: February 22, 2009 to June 26, 2010

3rd 70...**to seal the purification from sins**
Bush II: February 4, 2001 to June 8, 2002
Obama: June 27, 2010 to October 29, 2011

4th 70...**to make atonement for iniquity**
Bush II: June 9, 2002 – October 11, 2003
Obama: October 30, 2011 to March 2, 2013

5th 70...**to bring in everlasting righteousness**
Bush II: October 12, 2003 to February 12, 2005
Obama: March 3, 2013 to July 5, 2014

6th 70...**to seal the vision and prophecy**
Bush II: February 13, 2005 to June 17, 2006
Obama: July 6, 2014 to November 7, 2015

7th 70...**to anoint the Sanctuary**
Bush II: June 18, 2006 to October 20, 2007
Obama: November 8, 2015 to March 11, 2017

Trust God

I, Daniel, was mourning three full weeks. I ate no food...until three whole weeks were fulfilled...the twenty-fourth day of the first month (Daniel 10:2-4, MKJV).

Daniel understood from Jeremiah, the "Scripture of truth," that the 70 years of Jerusalem's desolation had ended when King Cyrus, the Prince of Persia, began to reign. Thus, Daniel had fasted and prayed for "three full weeks" in the first month that God would restore the sacrificial services in Jerusalem's Temple. Daniel's anguish, which overwhelmed him, did not cause him to sin. In his youth, Daniel was willing to die to obey God's dietary commands. When he was old, he did not forsake his faithfulness to God!

The prophet Daniel was an example of true sanctification. His long life was filled up with noble service for his Master. He was a man "greatly beloved" [Daniel 10:11] of Heaven. Yet instead of claiming to be pure and holy, this honored prophet identified himself with the really sinful of Israel, as he pleaded before God in behalf of his people: "We do not present our supplications before Thee for our righteousnesses, but for Thy great mercies." "We have sinned, we have done wickedly." He declares, "I was speaking, and praying, and confessing my sin and the sin of my people." And when at a later time the Son of God appeared, to give him instruction, he declares, "My comeliness was turned in me into corruption, and I retained no strength." [Daniel 9:18, 15, 20; 10:8] (GC88 470.3).

We do not understand as we should the great conflict going on between invisible agencies, the controversy between loyal and disloyal angels. Evil angels are constantly at work, planning their line of attack, controlling as commanders, kings, and rulers, the disloyal human forces... Do not indulge in fanciful speculations. The written Word is our only safety. We must pray as did Daniel, that we may be guarded by heavenly intelligences. As ministering spirits, angels are sent forth to minister to those who shall be heirs of salvation. *Pray, my brethren, pray as you have never prayed before. We are not prepared for the Lord's coming. We need to make thorough work for eternity* (4BC 1173.7).

The Hebrew lunar calendar starts with Nissan. But the first day of the seventh month (Tishrei) is New Year's Day. Nissan counts from the Exodus. Tishrei counts from earth's creation. Daniel fasted until the 24th of the *First Month,* but he would not have fasted during Passover, Nissan 14.

It shall be *the first month of the year...* Your lamb shall be without blemish...the *fourteenth day of the same month:* and the whole assembly of the congregation of Israel...*shall eat the flesh...* (cf Exodus 12:1-11).

The man that...forbeareth to keep the Passover ...shall bear his sin (cf Numbers 9:13).

Daniel's fast was in Tishrei, or according to God's word as it applied to His people in Daniel's Day, Daniel's fast would have been a sin. The first two days of Tishrei are one long day feast day: Rosh Hashanah (Jewish New Year). They begin the Ten Days of Awe in preparation for Yom Kippur, the Day of Atonement that aligns with September-October on the Gregorian calendar, when God's faithful people would have searched their souls in regards to their violating the Ten Commandments. Daniel fasted for *three weeks,* 21 days from Tishrei 3 thru the 24th *linking* his fast *to* the cleansing of the Temple on Yom Kippur. Immediately after Daniel's fast, Gabriel's coming to him on Tishrei 24 fits the context that aligns with Daniel's mourning about the desolation of the Sanctuary in Jerusalem and its suspended Services that were symbolic of making atonement for his sins.

Under the Mosaic system the cleansing of the sanctuary, or the great Day of Atonement, occurred on the tenth day of the seventh Jewish month (Leviticus 16:29-34), when the high priest, having made an atonement for all Israel, and thus removed their sins from the sanctuary, came forth and blessed the people (Great Controversy, page 399 paragraph 4).

While Daniel fasted, Gabriel worked with King Cyrus. "From the first day that thou didst set thine heart to understand, and to chasten thyself before thy God, thy words were heard... But the prince of the kingdom of Persia withstood me *one and twenty days*" (Daniel 10:12-13). The elderly Daniel, who was weakened by fasting, collapsed.

So great was the divine glory revealed to Daniel that he could not endure the sight. Then the messenger of Heaven veiled the brightness of his presence and appeared to the prophet as "one like the similitude of the sons of men." By his divine power he strengthened this man of integrity and of faith, to hear the message sent to him from God (RH, February 8, 1881 par. 32).

When our brethren and ministers shall feel the burden that should rest upon them, they will not be content with a few surface truths. They will sink the shaft deep, and will have the spirit that Daniel possessed. There will be no frivolous spirit: no cheap, superficial sanctification, prated from unsanctified lips, and coming from hearts that are destitute of purity, of consecration and wholehearted surrender to God. *There will be earnest prayer that the truth may be so indelibly stamped upon the heart that the entire man may be brought, with all his ways, into conformity to the truth.* "With the heart man believeth unto righteousness; and with the mouth confession is made unto salvation" (Romans 10:10, Manuscript Release Vol. 9, p. 365.2).

It cannot now be said by the Lord's servants, as it was by the prophet Daniel: "The time appointed was long." Daniel 10:1. It is now but a short time till the witnesses for God will have done their work in preparing the way of the Lord (Testimonies Vol. 6, p. 406 par. 4).

The book of Daniel is unsealed in the revelation to John, and it carries us forward to the last scenes of this earth's history (CTr 334.5).

In the Revelation, the Lion of the tribe of Judah has opened to the students of prophecy the book of Daniel, and thus is *Daniel* standing in his place. He *bears his testimony, that which the Lord revealed to him in vision, of the great and solemn events that we must know as we stand on the very threshold of their fulfillment* (Manuscript Release Vol. 17, p. 10 par. 2).

[Christ] opened the seal that closed the book of divine instruction. The world was permitted to gaze upon pure, unadulterated truth. Truth itself descended to roll back the darkness and counteract error...as a light shining in a dark place (Spalding and Magan Collection, p. 58.5).

Jesus identified Daniel as a prophet (cf Matthew 24:15; Mark 13:14). John is the revelator. Daniel's prophecies are unsealed by John in the Revelation. Especially in these last days, God wants us to understand the book of Daniel and Revelation's explanation, as His word says: "The Revelation of Jesus Christ, which God gave unto Him, to show unto His servants things which must shortly come to pass" (Revelation 1:1). The things that God *has opened to the students of prophecy in the book of Daniel* are supposed to be understood. In spite of our best efforts to study the Bible, our conclusions are not always correct and may be tainted by presumptions.

It was believed that Christ, our great High Priest, would appear to purify the earth by the destruction of sin and sinners, and to bless His waiting people with immortality. The tenth day of the seventh month, the great Day of Atonement, the time of the cleansing of the sanctuary, which in the year 1844 fell upon the twenty-second of October, was regarded as the time of the Lord's coming. This was in harmony with the proofs already presented that the 2300 days would terminate in the autumn, and the conclusion seemed irresistible (Great Controversy, page 399 paragraph 4).

Are we to wait until the fulfillment of the prophecies of the end before we say anything concerning them? Of what value will our words be then? Shall we wait until God's judgments fall upon the transgressor before we tell him how to avoid them? Where is our faith in the word of God? Must we see things foretold come to pass before we will believe what He has said? In clear, distinct rays light has come to us, showing us that the great day of the Lord is near at hand, "even at the doors." Let us read and understand before it is too late (9T 20.1).

Babylon besieged Jerusalem in 605 BC, the 3rd year of Jehoiakim's reign, when God gave it to Nebuchadnezzar (cf Daniel 1:1-2). Jeremiah prophesied, "*After seventy years* be accomplished at Babylon, I will visit you...to return to this place" (Jeremiah 29:10). In 535, "Cyrus succeeded to the throne, and the beginning of his reign marked the completion of the seventy years" (PK 556.4), but the Temple was in ruins, and the Jews had not returned to their homeland. The Lord had also said; "*I will bring them again into their land...first I will recompense their iniquity and their sin double*" (Jeremiah 16:15, 18). From 605, the 70 years doubled (140 years) ended in 465, King Artaxerxes' ascension year. He issued the final decree to rebuild Jerusalem and the Temple in his 7th year, 457 BC. Notice that Ezra "came to Jerusalem" that very year "in the fifth month, which [was] in the seventh year of the king...on the first [day] of the fifth month..." (Ezra 7:8-9).

Jerusalem fell	605 BC
70 years	-70 years
Jeremiah's 70 years ended	535 BC
70 years doubled (140 years)	-70 years
Temple built/Captivity ends	465 BC

For prophetic calculations, a year has 360 days: the 2300 days of Daniel 8:14 divided by 360 are 6 years, 4 months, and 20 days. Thus, the local fulfillment of Daniel's 2300-day prophecy, aligns with Ezra's arrival in Jerusalem in the 7th year, on the 1st day of the 5th month, after King Artaxerxes had ruled 6 years 4 months! A brief tarrying time was foretold in Habakkuk 2:3; the rebuilt Sanctuary was cleansed on the 457 BC Day of Atonement. But Ezekiel linked the Temple's destruction to *longtime*: A day for a year: "I have appointed thee each day for a year" (Ezekiel 4:6). A few years after that prediction, the Temple was destroyed when Nebuchadnezzar "burnt the house of the LORD" (2 Kings 25:9). As it had been destroyed in fulfillment of a *longtime* (a day = a year) prophecy, the prophecy of its cleansing must be fulfilled in *long-time*. The 457 BC *cleansing of the Sanctuary* did not completely fulfill Daniel 8:14 in *long-time*, thus, it began the countdown to 1843.

Calculation of the time was so simple and plain that even the children could understand it. From the date of the decree of the king of Persia, found in Ezra 7, which was given in 457 before Christ, the 2300 years of Daniel 8:14 must terminate with 1843. Accordingly, we looked to the end of this year for the coming of the Lord. We were sadly disappointed when the year entirely passed away and the Saviour had not come (LS80 185.2).

"The 1843 chart was directed by the hand of the Lord, and that it should not be altered; that the figures were as He wanted them" (ExV 61.1).

Misapprehension of this...brought disappointment and perplexity to those who had fixed upon the earlier date as the time of the Lord's coming. But this did not in the least affect the strength of the argument showing that the 2300 days terminated in the year 1844, and that the great event represented by the cleansing of the sanctuary must then take place (GC88 328.3).

The prophetic periods reached to 1844, and that the same evidence they had presented to show that the prophetic periods closed in 1843, proved that they would terminate in 1844 (1SG 138.1).

The details of the *long-time prophecy*, 2300-years (Daniel 8:14), are specified in Daniel 11. It began with *three kings in Persia* (11:2): Cyrus, Darius, and Artaxerxes (cf Ezra 6:14). Their decrees ended the 2300 literal day prophecy in 457 BC; thus, began the 2300-years (Ezra 5:13; 7:21, 26). After the 2300-day/year prophecy ended in 457 BC, in 1843 and in 1844 AD, it is clear that this is a dual prophecy with multiple meanings. The 1843 ending date aligns with Old Testament prophecies, while the 1844 date aligns with New Testament prophecies. Michael stood for His people (Daniel 12:1) to cleanse Heaven's Temple at the beginning of the Investigative Judgment in 1844: "He that overcometh...I will not blot out his name out of the book of life, but I will confess his name before My Father, and before His angels." "And behold, I come quickly; and My reward is with Me, to give every man according as his work shall be" (Revelation 3:5; 22:12).

After the great disappointment in 1844, Satan and his angels were busily engaged in laying snares to unsettle the faith of the body. He was affecting the minds of individuals who had a personal experience in these things. They had an appearance of humility. They changed the first and second messages, and pointed to the future for their fulfillment, while others pointed far back in the past, declaring that they had been there fulfilled. These individuals were drawing the minds... away, and unsettling their faith. Some were searching the Bible to try to build up a faith of their own, independent of the body. Satan exulted in all this; for he knew that those who broke loose from the anchor, he could affect by different errors and drive about with winds of doctrine. *Many who had led in the first and second messages, denied them,* and division and scattering was throughout the body. I then saw Wm. Miller. He looked perplexed, and was bowed with sorrow and distress for his people. He saw the company who were united and loving in 1844, losing their love for each other, and opposing one another. He saw them fall back into a cold, backslidden state. Grief wasted his strength. I saw leading men watching Wm. Miller, and fearing lest he should embrace the third angel's message and the commandments of God. And as he would lean towards the light from heaven...human influence exerted to keep his mind in darkness, and to retain his influence among them. At length Wm. Miller raised his voice against the light from heaven. He failed in not receiving the message which would have fully explained his disappointment, and cast a light and glory on the past, which would have revived his exhausted energies, brightened up his hope, and led him to glorify God. But he leaned to human wisdom instead of divine, and being broken with arduous labor in his Master's cause, and by age, he was not as accountable as those who kept him from the truth. They are responsible, and the sin rests upon them. If Wm. Miller could have seen the light of the third message, many things which looked dark and mysterious to him would have been explained... His heart would incline towards the truth; but then he looked at his brethren. They opposed it. Could he tear away from those who had stood side and shoulder with him in proclaiming Jesus' coming? He thought they surely would not lead him astray (Spiritual Gifts Vol. 1, p. 166 par. 1).

Today in Prophecy

When the prophetic events begun by the three Persian kings in 457 BC that are detailed in Daniel 11 reached the 1844 Investigative Judgment, the prophecy (Daniel 11:1-45) was fulfilled. "Jesus rose up, and shut the door, and entered the Holy of Holies, at the 7th month 1844; but Michael's standing up (Daniel 12:1) *to deliver His people, is in the future*" (Word to the Little Flock, page 12 paragraph 4).

Daniel 11:40-45 had predicted what was to take place immediately before Christ stood to start the Investigative Judgment. William Miller had understood that the *Kings of the North and South* had become European powers. He linked them to "*Spain, in the south, and Great Britain, in the north...*" Then "Spain...joined the *French*" (Evidence From Scripture and History of the Second Coming of Christ About the year 1843, William Miller (1841) p. 105). Miller was partly correct.

Claiming to be the Ottoman's friend, France invaded Egypt, an Ottoman province, to become the King of the South. Simultaneously, "a French army entered Rome, and made the pope a prisoner" (GC88 266.2). "Pius VI...the pope specified in prophecy, which received the deadly wound" (5MR 318.1). "*One of his heads* as it were wounded to death" (Revelation 13:3); a head on this beast depicts *a pope*.

With the French fleet dominating the Mediterranean and its ports, Admiral Nelson harbored the British fleet near the fortress at Gibraltar until he located the French fleet. He crossed the Mediterranean in 30 days (whirlwind speed for sailing ships). "And at the time of the end shall the king of the south push at him: and the king of the north shall come against him like a whirlwind, with chariots, and with horsemen, and with many ships" (Daniel 11:40). Nelson sank the French fleet off the coast of Egypt in the battle at Abuqir August 1, 1798. Then, without his fleet, Napoleon attempted to go back to Europe over land. On the way, he besieged Acre (Akka), a strategic Ottoman fortress between Egypt and Syria. Joining forces with the Ottomans, the

British shelled the French positions. Prophetically, Britain became the King of the North. Napoleon retreated to Egypt with the British pursuing him as Daniel had prophesied:

> He shall enter also into the glorious land, and many countries shall be overthrown: but these shall escape out of his hand, even Edom, and Moab, and the chief of the children of Ammon. He shall stretch forth his hand also upon the countries: and the land of Egypt shall not escape (Daniel 11:41-42).

Napoleon returned to Egypt (without fighting in Jordan, Moab, or Edom); he escaped with his army to Europe. The British then dominated the Mideast to secure their routes to India. "He shall have power over the treasures of gold and of silver, and over all the precious things of Egypt: and the Libyans and the Ethiopians shall be at his steps." "Tidings out of the east and out of the north shall trouble him: therefore, he shall go forth with great fury to destroy, and utterly to make away many" (11:43, 44). Britain was fighting in the *east* and the *north*: 1803-India, 1812-USA, and 1815France (Waterloo, 11:40). Henry John Temple, 3rd Viscount Palmerston, Britain's Foreign Secretary, feared a Russian-French alliance would shift the European balance of power. He also feared that Russia in the *north* would expand into India through Afghanistan. He used the Ottoman Empire as a barrier to keep Russia from accessing the Mediterranean. Palmerston convinced Russia, Prussia, and Austria July 15, 1840 that Egypt was about to overthrow the Ottoman Empire. He preferred a weak sultan rather than a strong military leader that would strengthen and enlarge the Ottoman Empire. On August 11, 1840, they gave Egypt an ultimatum to stand down or face their allied forces. Muhammad Ali of Egypt refused, and war followed.

Daniel 11:45 literally states: *To plant dwelling palace sea glorious holy mountain to come end of time to help.* The British fleet placed itself on the sea between Mount Carmel and Acre, which it occupied in 1840. "In the face of European military might, Muhammad Ali acquiesced" (www.en.wikipedia.org). Palmerston's government *came to its end* in 1841 when it was voted out of office. Some have observed that Queen Victoria was delighted to see him and his *gun boat diplomacy* go.

Some of these prophecies were understood before they were fulfilled. "Josiah Litch in 1838, two years before the expected event was to occur. In that year he predicted that the Turkish power would be overthrown "in A.D. 1840, sometime in the month of August;" [Josiah Litch, The Probability of the Second Coming of Christ About A.D. 1843, p. 157] "but a few days before the fulfillment of the prophecy he concluded more definitely from his study that the period allotted to the Turks would come to an end on August 11, 1840" (Daniel and the Revelation, Uriah Smith, p. 513).

In 1844, fulfilled prophecy was linked to the command, "Take *it*, and eat it up [Daniel 11]; and it shall make thy belly bitter [the Great Disappointment], but it shall be in thy mouth sweet as honey [the proclamation of Christ's Advent]" (Revelation 10:9, supplemented). Then came the command: "*Thou must prophesy again*" (Revelation 10:11). Who is to *prophesy again*? The prophet Daniel; chapter 11 is to *prophesy again*: To repeat. But the repeating of the prophetic history is not linked to *long-time*, i.e., a day for a year: "*Time shall be no longer*" (Revelation 10:6). Daniel 11 repeats the prophetic history without linking these events to a definite duration of time. After the prophetic history in Daniel 11 ended in 1844, the prophecy begins to repeat at Daniel 11:6.

> And in the end of years, they shall join themselves together; for the king's daughter of the south shall come to the king of the north to make an agreement: but she shall not retain the power of the arm; neither shall he stand, nor his arm: but she shall be given up, and they that brought her, and he that begat her, and he that strengthened her in [these] times (Daniel 11:6).

"A woman, representing the Lord's chosen church" (RH, February 26, 1914, par. 7). France had assumed the role as the *Protector of the Catholics*, Christ's former Church. The Tsar protested that the Orthodox Christians in Palestine were oppressed by the French backed Catholics, and the Crimean War (1854-1856) followed, in which *France and England joined themselves*. Count Cavour, who was unifying Italy under King Victor Emanuel II joined the allies in time to participate in the peace talks. He resolved a disputed border between France and Italy that set Italian unification in motion. The pope opposed unification because he would lose secular rule over the *Papal States*. But though British warships were off Italy's coast to evacuate her nationals, if needed, during the fight for unification, neither England nor France helped the papacy to keep the Papal States.

By 1870, "France was stripped of its Italian territories... Meanwhile, the Italian king had driven the pope into the Vatican City and was thereafter excommunicated from the Catholic Church" (www.heritage-history.com). Italy became the King of the South (then specifically Mussolini).

> But out of a branch of her roots shall [one] stand up in his estate, which shall come with an army, and <u>shall enter into the fortress of the king of the north</u>, and shall deal against them, <u>and shall prevail</u>. And shall also carry captives into Egypt their gods, with their princes, [and] with their precious vessels of silver and of gold; and <u>he shall continue [more] years than the king of the north</u> (Daniel 11:7-8).

The Roman Church's roots were the religious (church) and secular (state). In 1922, the king of the south, Mussolini (*a branch of the state/political roots*) seized Italy's government that had formed alliances (1885-1889) with the African kingdoms: Obbia, Zanzibar, and Caluula. He unilaterally seized the Jubaland Province of Kenya and the town and port of Kismayo from Britain in spite of official borders that existed between Italian Somaliland and Kenya since 1908.

England relinquished the territory to Italy (cf www. bearcats). Italy's influence spread to Ethiopia and the colonial Italian Empire expanded toward Egypt (www.en. wikipedia.org). In WWII, Britain alleged that Egypt's Prime Minister favored the Axis powers. King Farouk I was given the ultimatum to replace him or be replaced. The king reportedly told Britain's Ambassador that he would get rid of his *Italian advisors* when the ambassador got rid of his *Italian advisor* (his wife). After World War II, Egypt's British trained generals ousted King Farouk. He was granted asylum in Italy. But during the war, when Britain had been about to fall to the Axis powers, President Roosevelt (FDR) became the King of the North. "He shall continue [more] years than the king of the north" (Daniel 11:8). Mussolini began to rule in 1922, when he seized Italy's government, and he died April 28, 1945. The King of the South continued longer than FDR, who had become President in 1933 and died April 12, 1945.

> Each Gospel is a supplement to the others, every prophecy an explanation of another, every truth a development of some other truth (Education, p. 123).

> In the prophecies, the future is opened before us as plainly as it was opened...by the words of Christ. *The events...are clearly presented. But multitudes have no more understanding of these important truths than if they had never been revealed* (GC88 594.1).

Thus, the prophecies in Daniel 11 continue to align with the history that it predicts. "So, the king of the south shall... return into his own land" (Daniel 11:9), from Italy to Egypt. "His sons shall be stirred up...then shall he return, and be stirred up, [even] to his fortress" (11:10). America's fortress was Israel. After the *Jews Returned in 1948,* Egypt *assembled a multitude of forces* against Israel. "He shall set forth a great multitude; but the multitude shall be given into his hand (11:11). Egypt with the Arab League *made multiple attempts* to move against America's fortress. But the UN kept the peace until the funding ceased. Egypt invaded Israel: The 1967 six-day war fulfilled this prophecy. "He shall cast down [many] ten thousands: but he shall not be strengthened [by it]" (11:12). "1973, Yom Kippur...Egyptian and Syrian armies launched a surprise attack against Israel" (www.en. wikipedia.org). After Egypt's Sadat made peace with Israel, the King of the South transitioned to his former ally, Hussein. "The king of the north shall return" (Daniel 11:13-14). Bush I, King of the North, who had envisioned the New World Order of "peace and security, freedom, and the rule of law" (www.infoplease.com) rallied the world against Iraq. After Bush I fought Hussein, the King of the South changed to Osama (Usama) bin Laden, "who in 1998 declared holy war on America" (www.msnbc.msn.com). The King of the North, President Clinton, attacked bin Laden (cf Daniel 11:15). The King of the South reverted to Iraq, who Clinton also attacked in 1998. After Daniel's narration arrives at 1998, the prophecy tells what led up to the conflict:

> So, the king of the north shall come, and cast up a mount, and take the most fenced cities: and the arms of the south shall not withstand, neither his chosen people, neither [shall there be any] strength to withstand. But he that cometh against him shall do according to his own will, and none shall stand before him: and he shall stand in the glorious land, which by his hand shall be consumed. He shall also set his face to enter with the strength of his whole kingdom, and upright ones with him; thus, shall he do: and he shall give him the daughter of women, corrupting her: but she shall not stand [on his side], neither be for him. After this shall he turn his face unto the isles, and shall take many: but a prince for his own behalf shall cause the reproach offered by him to cease; without his own reproach he shall cause [it] to turn upon him. Then he shall turn his face toward the

fort of his own land: but <u>he shall stumble and fall, and not be found</u> (Daniel 11:15-19).

October 26-29, 1994...Clinton attended the signing of the Israel-Jordan peace agreement [in Israel] ... And spoke to the Knesset in Jerusalem (<u>www.state.gov</u>).

Who gave *the daughter of women* to Clinton? Unlike the daughter of the King of the south (1798 papacy, Daniel 11:6), this was Monica Lewinsky. "May 5-8, 1995 Prime Minister Yitzhak Rabin Israel Met with President Clinton during a private visit" (<u>www.state.gov</u>). Clinton's "inappropriate relationship" with Lewinsky was in 1995. She is of Jewish descent (<u>www.en.wikipedia.org</u>). "Monica will go down in history as the woman who had sex with an American president and saved an Israeli prime minister" (<u>www. meforum.org</u>). She did *not stand on Clinton's* side when she produced that infamous dress. *The glorious <u>land</u> was consumed. Land:* comes from a root that links to *a moral sense: the impurity of lustful...profligate living* (cf Strong). While the US was *consumed* with Clinton's scandal. He stood in the *glorious land* pushing the peace process! "November 4, 1995, Rabin was assassinated... leaving a mass rally in Tel Aviv in support of the Oslo process" (<u>www.en.wikipedia.org</u>). In <u>Living History</u>, Hillary Clinton has a photo of President Clinton's return to Israel for Rabin's funeral with *upright ones with him*: Gingrich and Dole. *He then went to the British Isles* (<u>www.state.gov</u>). "The December 1998 bombing of Iraq (code-named Operation Desert Fox)" (<u>www.en.wikipedia.org</u>) redirected public focus to Iraq. The House of Representatives impeached Clinton. He apologized. The Republican Senate acquitted him. *He caused it to turn upon*: Gingrich, the prince in America's line of succession, who resigned (Daniel 11:18).

Then shall stand up <u>in his estate</u> a raiser of taxes [in] the glory of the kingdom: but within few days he shall be [broken], neither in anger, nor in battle...And <u>in his estate</u> shall stand up a vile person, to whom they shall not give the honour of the kingdom: but <u>he shall come in</u> <u>peaceably, and obtain the kingdom by flatteries</u>...and shall be broken; yea, also the prince of the covenant...he shall work deceitfully: for he shall...become strong (Daniel 11:20-23).

Estate is *foot* most of the times it is in the Bible. The end time image in Daniel 2 has Reagan as the head of gold, Bush I as the silver, Clinton as the brass, Bush II as one iron leg, Obama as the other, Trump as a *foot* of iron and clay, and America's last President as the 2nd *foot*. Daniel 11: 20-23 goes directly from Bush II to the last President: The 2nd foot linking to Daniel 2 that shall *be broken* at Christ's Coming. Meanwhile, 11:25-27 states that the kings of the North and South *tell lies at one table*. Bush II Lied about *not wanting war* and Saddam lied about WMD's. Obama's nuclear deal with Iran was a lie that Trump trashed. Will the US and Iran make another doomed deal before the Biden-Harris administration turns "against the holy covenant" (11:28)?

> This power, the last that is to wage war against the church and the law of God, is represented by a beast with lamblike horns. The beasts preceding it had risen from the sea; but this came up out of the earth...it symbolized—the United States (ST, Feb 8, 1910, par. 5).

> We have no time to lose. Troublous times are before us. The world is stirred with the spirit of war. Soon the scenes of trouble spoken of in the prophecies will take place. The prophecy in the eleventh of Daniel has nearly reached its complete fulfillment. *Much of the <u>history</u> that has taken place <u>in fulfillment of this prophecy will be repeated</u>.* In the thirtieth verse a power is spoken of that "shall be grieved, and return, and have indignation against the holy covenant: so, shall he do; he shall even return, and have intelligence with them that forsake the holy covenant" [Verses 31-36, quoted] (13MR 394.1).

He Is Coming!

The day of the Lord is approaching with stealthy tread; but the supposed great and wise men know not the signs of Christ's coming or of the end of the world. (Testimonies Vol. 6, page 406 paragraph 6).

Those who commune with God walk in the light of the Sun of Righteousness. *They do not dishonor their Redeemer by corrupting their way before God.* Heavenly light shines upon them. <u>As they near the close of this earth's history, their knowledge of Christ, and of the prophecies relating to Him, greatly increases.</u> ...They are in unity with His Son. To them the word of God is of surpassing beauty and loveliness. They see its importance. Truth is unfolded to them. The doctrine of the incarnation is invested with a soft radiance. They see that <u>the Scripture is the key that unlocks all mysteries and solves all difficulties</u>. *Those who have been unwilling to receive the light and walk in the light will be unable to understand the mystery of godliness, but those who have not hesitated to take up the cross and follow Jesus, will see light in God's light* (SW, April 4, 1905, paragraph 10).

Satan is fast obtaining the control of human minds who have not the fear of God before them. Let all <u>read and understand the prophecies of this book</u> [Daniel], <u>for we are now entering upon the time of trouble spoken of</u>: *"And at that time shall Michael stand up, the great prince which standeth for the children of thy people: and there shall be a <u>time of trouble</u>, such as never was since there was a nation [even] to that same time: and at that time thy people shall be delivered, every one that shall be found written in the book. And many of them that sleep in the dust of the earth shall awake, some to everlasting life, and some to shame [and] everlasting contempt. And they that be wise shall shine as the brightness of the* firmament; and they that turn many to righteousness as the stars forever and ever. But thou, O <u>Daniel, shut up the words, and seal the book, [even] to the time of the end: many shall run to and fro, and *knowledge shall be increased*</u>" [Daniel 12:1-4] (13MR 394.2).

Precious, vital truths, are bound up with man's eternal well-being both in this life and in the eternity that is opening before us. "Sanctify them through Thy truth: Thy word is truth" John 17:17 (7T 249.1).

Michael standing for His people in Daniel 12:1 is Christ standing for His saints. Matthew Henry knew it: "Michael is simply another of the many names for Jesus Himself" (<u>www.amazingfacts.org</u>). Jesus stood for His people in 1844, but that did not start the Time of Trouble, thus, His standing for His people in 1844 is not the complete fulfillment of 12:1.

"<u>The commencement of that time of trouble,</u>" here <u>mentioned does not refer to the time when the plagues shall begin to be poured out, but to a short period just before they are poured out, while Christ is in the sanctuary</u>. At that time, while the work of salvation is closing, trouble will be coming on the earth, and the nations will be angry, yet held in check so as not to prevent the work of the third angel. At that time the "latter rain," or refreshing from the presence of the Lord, will come, to give power to the loud voice of the third angel, and prepare the saints to stand in the period when the seven last plagues shall be poured out (EW 85.3).

<u>Michael</u> had not stood up [and put on His vengeance garments], and that the <u>time of trouble</u>, such as never was, had not yet commenced. The nations are now getting angry, but when our High Priest has finished His work in the sanctuary, He <u>will stand up, put on the garments of vengeance, and then the seven last plagues will be poured out</u> (Early Writings p. 36.1).

Though Jesus has not stood to don vengeance garments, He stood to confess us before His Father and His angels in 1844. He continued to stand for us thru the Judgment Hours, 83-years 4-months each, of the dead and living. And He will stand to come for us, when "It is done": The judgment will be over; the seven last plagues will begin. This being true, I had difficulty understanding how Michael standing to begin the Time of Trouble, *just before the plagues are poured out*, refers to Jesus, who stands to begin the plagues. From Daniel 10:13, I knew that Michael, *is one of the chief princes.* Thus, I anticipated that President Trump would be broken (out of office: By being impeached, or by some mechanism) and that as Isaiah had prophesied of King Cyrus, I read Daniel to be saying that Michael Pence would stand as President: To begin the Time of Trouble. It did not happen; but by faith, I believed it until President Biden was in office. I was mistaken, about President Michael Pence following Trump. Satan, who *wants to be like God* (Michael) stands for his people to begin the Time of Trouble. Thus, the prophecy in Revelation is clear: The 7 heads on the papal-beast that symbolized the post-1929 popes have ruled until Pope Benedict XVI, when the prophecy shifted to the earth-beast with *duo* lamblike horns, symbolizing four US Presidents. Three have ruled: Bush II, Obama, and Trump. The fourth President, who is in office on March 29, 2021, is the last American President that Bible prophecy identifies!

The date is significant, because Revelation 18 is about the end time fall of <u>Babylon</u>. Starting with President Washington, American Presidents began their term in March. By Babylonian reckoning, Babylon's kings began reigning on New Year's Day (March 29th on our Gregorian calendar). When Babylon's king died, the new king's Ascension Year was counted as the balance of the old king's final year. The new king's reign officially began on March 29. In fallen Babylon, Pope John-Paul II died April 2, 2005, a few days after March 29. By Babylonian tradition, Pope Benedict XVI completed Pope John-Paul II's final year until March 29,

2006, when Benedict's first year began. He resigned effective February 28, 2013, one month and one day short of 7 years, i.e., a short space: *"The number 7 indicates <u>completeness</u>, and is symbolic of the fact that <u>the messages extend to the end of time</u>"* (AA 585.3). If Kamala [6] Harris [6] Emhoff [6] ever becomes President after March 29, 2021, it will be as though she was never President because Joe Biden has fulfilled the prophecy to become America's last *Prince of the Constitution*, the 4th horn identified in Revelation 13's prophecy. Will President Biden rely on Kamala as if she were a coruler? How she relates to the 666 Mark of the Beast will be revealed! Then Michael (Christ) stands to begin the seven last plagues.

When the third angel's message closes, mercy no longer pleads for the guilty inhabitants of the earth. The people of God have accomplished their work. They have received "the latter rain," "the refreshing from the presence of the Lord," and they are prepared for the trying hour before them. Angels are hastening to and fro in heaven. An angel returning from the earth announces that his work is done; the final test has been brought upon the world, and *all who have proved themselves loyal to the divine precepts have received "the seal of the living God."* Then Jesus ceases His intercession in the sanctuary above. He lifts His hands and with a loud voice says, "It is done;" and all the angelic host lay off their crowns as He makes the solemn announcement: "He that is unjust, let him be unjust still: and he which is filthy, let him be filthy still: and he that is righteous, let him be righteous still: and he that is holy, let him be holy still." Revelation 22:11. Every case has been decided for life or death. Christ has made the atonement for His people and blotted out their sins (Great Controversy p. 613 par. 2).

In the last days, the "ships of Chittim shall come against him" (Daniel 11:30), i.e., attack America's fleet. *Chittim* denotes Cyprus. It links to *"islanders of the Mediterranean*

Sea; the descendants of Javan" (cf Strong). Javan is "the generic name of the Greek race" (Easton's Bible Dictionary). The Island of Cyprus was included in the Greek empire that extended to Iran, which has islands: End time Chittim. <u>Iran has a plan</u>. Will a US-Iranian war morph into Armageddon?

The <u>Iranian Navy locked its missiles on an American aircraft carrier</u>...and detained two US Navy boats...in Iranian territorial waters... (<u>http://www.liveleak.com</u>).

[Iran's] Navy has received **340** <u>stealthy speedboats... capable of carrying various types of rockets to attack enemy targets</u> (<u>www.defenseworld.net</u>).

<u>Iran will target American aircraft carriers in the Persian Gulf should a war between the two countries ever break out</u> ... "Aircraft carriers are the symbol of America's military might" ... "The carriers are responsible for supplying America's air power. So, it's natural that we want to sink the carriers." ... "<u>the Nimitz-class carriers used by the United States could be seriously damaged or destroyed if 24 missiles were fired simultaneously</u>" (<u>www.columbiatribune.com</u>).

Now, just now, it is time for us to be watching, working, and waiting. *The word of the Lord reveals the fact that the end of all things is at hand, and its testimony is most decided that it is necessary for every soul to have the truth planted in the heart so that it will control the life and sanctify the character.* The Spirit of the Lord is working to take the truth of the inspired word and stamp it upon the soul so that the professed followers of Christ will have a holy, sacred joy that they will be able to impart to others. The opportune time for us to work is now, just now, while the day lasts. But there is no command for anyone to search the Scripture in order to ascertain, if possible, when probation will close. God has no such message for any mortal lips. He would have no mortal tongue declare that which He has hidden in His secret councils (Review and Herald, October 9, 1894, par. 11).

Transgression has almost reached its limit. Confusion fills the world, and a great terror is soon to come upon human beings. The end is very near. We who know the truth should be preparing for what is soon to break upon the world as an overwhelming surprise (Testimony Vol. 8, page 28 paragraph 1).

While it was not given to the prophets to understand fully the things revealed to them, they earnestly sought to obtain all the light which God had been pleased to make manifest (Great Controversy, page 344 paragraph 3).

The meaning was to be unfolded, from age to age, as the people of God should need the instruction therein contained (Great Controversy 1888, p. 344 par. 1).

From the condition of things in our world, we can see that we are...in the last days (www.egwwritings.org).

The light that Daniel received direct from God was given especially for these last days. The visions he saw by the banks of the Ulai and the Hiddekel...are now in process of fulfillment, and all the events foretold will soon have come to pass (4BC 1166.5).

"*By the side of the...Hiddekel...*Michael, one of the chief princes, came to help me" (Daniel 10:4, 13). Michael: "Who is like God." Lucifer wanted to be "like the Most High" (Isaiah 14:14). The war in Heaven was between *Michael and the dragon* (Lucifer, cf Revelation 12:7). "Satan...attempted...— to deceive and destroy the people by palming off upon them a counterfeit in place of the true." "He will stir up the wicked to destroy God's people in the time of trouble." "The wrath of Satan...and his work of deceit and destruction will reach its culmination in the time of trouble" (Great Controversy 1888, pp. 186.1, 618.2, 623.2). **"How long before Satan will, through his devices, again bring upon God's people a time of trouble? ...in the near future..."** (HS 242.3).

We are close to the time spoken of by Daniel the prophet (Manuscript Release Vol. 14, p. 136 par. 4).

Though Miller understood the *daily* as paganism, *daily* is translated as *continual* in 2 Kings 25:30. "From the time [that] the <u>*continual*</u> <daily> shall be <u>taken away</u>, and the <u>abomination that maketh desolate set up</u>, [there shall be] a thousand two hundred and ninety days" (Daniel 12:11). *When was the <u>continual</u> taken away?* "Power was given unto him to <u>continue</u> forty [and] two months" (Revelation 13:5). From 9/11/01, the *season and time* (Daniel 7:12), 1260 days later on February 22, 2005, Pope John-Paul II returned to the hospital to die: <u>His power was taken away</u>; he was not ruling church or state. From the time that the continual (Pope John-Paul II) was taken away (2/22/05), 1290 days count to September 4, 2008. "Understand the matter and consider the vision [*mareh* (what is seen)]," a blessing comes to him that waits 1335 days (cf Daniel 9:23; 12:12). Those days ended May 1, 2012, during the 4th end time 70 weeks allotted *to make atonement for iniquity* (10/30/11 to 3/2/13).

"Seventy weeks are determined upon thy people and upon thy holy city, to finish the transgression, and to make an end of sins, and to make <u>reconciliation for iniquity</u>, and to bring in everlasting righteousness, and to <u>seal up the vision and prophecy</u>, and to anoint the most Holy." "At the time appointed, he shall <u>return</u>...but it shall not be as the former, or as the latter" (Daniel 9:24; 11:29). The former and latter times, President Obama sent troops to fight in Afghanistan in 2009; 17,000 in February and 30,000 in December. On this return, President Obama personally went to Afghanistan; May 1, 2012, when he sealed the vision and the prophecy during these end time 70 weeks.

We are living in the time of the end. Thrones and churches have united to oppose God's purposes...It is the reign of Antichrist. God's law is set aside. The Scriptures are exchanged for the traditions of men. <u>Satan has become the ruler of the world</u>... (RH, Dec. 15, 1904, 1-2).

Every prophecy is an explanation of another. From May 1, 2012, Daniel's prophecies align with others and recent events. 1. "Another angel [has] come down from heaven, having great power; and the earth [is being] lightened with his glory" (Revelation 18:1). 2. Babylon is fallen because of her fornication: Benedict XVI resigned amidst the priests' fornication scandal and Pope Francis I supports same sex *civil unions* (18:2). 3. People (Euphrates, 16:12) flowing into papal Babylon is drying up. 4. February 14, 2013, Babylon's sins reached Heaven; the time allotted for the Judgment Hour of the living ended: God is preparing us for the Mark of the Beast that will separate His faithful servants from all others; reject Babylon's sins, flee from her, and avoid her judgments and plagues (18:4-5). 5. Pope Francis I's light show (www.youtube.com/watch?v=WtI6P9R3x4E, December 9, 2015) displayed St. Peter's Basilica as a cage of unclean birds (Revelation 18:2). 6. The US Supreme Court with a majority of Catholic trained justices drank the wine of Babylon's fornication when it ruled (June 26, 2015) that marriage now entails the priests' gay sex acts (between two men or between two women) as if it is the same as marriage between a man and a woman like God created it in the beginning (18:3). 6. President Obama, the earth-king, identified in prophecy first supported *gay marriage* May 9, 2012 and reaffirmed it in 2015, declaring the Supreme Court's decision: *A victory* (www.nytimes.com, Rev. 18:9).

Whenever the will of God is violated by nations or by individuals, a day of retribution comes, as surely as rivers that burst their banks carry devastation before them (Manuscript Release Vol. 19, p. 391 par. 2).

Flee Babylon!

An apostate church will unite with the powers of earth and hell to place upon the forehead or in the hand, the mark of the beast, and prevail upon the children of God to worship the beast and his image. They will seek to compel them to renounce their allegiance to God's law, and yield homage to the papacy (RH, Nov. 8, 1892, par. 7).

Babylon is fallen, is fallen, that great city, because she made all nations drink of the wine of the wrath of *her fornication...* Babylon the great is fallen, is fallen, and is become the habitation of devils, and the hold of every foul spirit, and a cage of every unclean and hateful bird. For all nations have drunk of the wine of the wrath of *her fornication, and the kings of the earth have committed fornication with her ... Come out of her, My people, that ye be not partakers of her sins, and that ye receive not of her plagues* (cf Revelation 14:8; 18:2-4).

"The term Babylon, derived from Babel, and signifying confusion, is applied in Scripture to the various forms of false or apostate religion" (4SP 232.2). It may be difficult for people, who believe that their church is true, to see that it is Babylon: Apostate Religion embracing the doctrines of devils. The media has exposed fornication scandals that reveal the churches' true spiritual condition! Pope Benedict resigned in the midst of the priests' sex scandal. Pope Francis is telling nations to legalize civil unions, *"What we have to have is a civil union law...I supported that"* www.americamagazine.org. *Fornicating* Babylon is fallen: *Come out of her My people!*

Before the coming of Christ, important developments in the religious world, foretold in prophecy, were to take place. The apostle declared: "Be not soon shaken in mind, or be troubled, neither by spirit, nor by word, nor by letter as from us, as that the day of Christ is at hand. Let no man deceive you by any means: for that day shall not come, except there come a falling away first" (AA 265.1).

God's word says that licentious heterosexuality and homosexuality are sins. As in Christ's day, leaders led God's people away from Him (the Light of the world), it is happening now in Apostate Christendom. Churches are indulging in Babylon's priests' fornication. June 12, 2019, the Southern Baptist Convention revealed that ministers in 750 of its churches have been abusing boys (www.bpnews.net). The Methodists, were on the verge of splitting over gay marriage (www.npr.org). Fornicating Babylon includes Islam and Judaism: "ISIS terrorists would tell the captives they had to rape them to convert them to Islam" and Jewish pedophiles find refuge in Israel (www.thesun.co.uk, www.cbsnews.com).

The churches' fornication scandals are *important developments in the religious world!* The falling away is here! Media reports confirm the Bible's prophetic warning: *Babylon is fallen because of her fornication.* In spite of the exposés, many people see nothing wrong with the Roman Church or her doctrines. Apostate Christendom is turning from sound doctrines to reunite with the fornicating mother Church. Truth is set aside for Babylon's fornication and the doctrines of devils. Her teachings on abortion and the male priesthood deceive others. Apostate zealots try to compel all to yield their conscience to the majority's *form of godliness*: Through compulsion they seek to abolish freedom of religion!

> "There is no real standard of righteousness apart from God's law. By obedience to this law the intellect is strengthened, and the conscience is enlightened and made sensitive." We "need to gain a clear understanding of God's law." We "are not left to follow blindly the guidance of men. The great prophetic waymarks which God Himself has set up show the path of obedience to be the only path that can be followed with certainty" (Youth Instructor, September 22, 1903, paragraph 8).

So, it will be again. The authorities will make laws to restrict religious liberty. They will assume the right that is God's alone. They will think they can force the conscience, which God alone should control. Even now they are making a beginning; this work they will continue to carry forward till they reach a boundary over which they cannot step. God will interpose in behalf of His loyal, commandment-keeping people (DA 630.1).

Shall we exalt human wisdom, and point to finite, changeable, erring men as a dependence in time of trouble? Or shall we exemplify our faith by our trust in God's power, revealing the net of false theories, religions, and philosophies which Satan has spread to catch unwary souls? (SpTA06 30.1)

Therein shall be left a remnant that shall be brought forth... and ye shall be comforted concerning the evil that I have brought upon Jerusalem, [even] concerning all that I have brought upon it (Ezekiel 14:22).

God will not compel anyone to obey Him! Nor will He shower blessings upon people, who persist in rebellion! In spite of God's great love for Israel, He allowed unspeakable chapters in their history: Babylonian Captivity, destruction of Jerusalem, Judaism's replacement by Christianity, and even the Holocaust. God's blessing and cursing of His chosen people, is an example that all nations and people must hear and heed. God's turning from those who turn from Him is a fact that Apostate Christianity will soon encounter. In the example of Noah's day: Professing faith (though sincere) did not save anyone who did not obey and enter the ark.

The dealings of God with His people should be often repeated. He has worked as a wonder-working God. He has baptized His chosen messengers with the Holy Spirit. The past history of the cause of God needs often to be brought before the people, young and old, that they may be familiar with it. How frequently were the waymarks set up by the Lord in His dealing with ancient Israel, lest they should forget the history of the past? (9MR 134.3)

Our salvation depends on a knowledge of the truth contained in the Scriptures. It is God's will that we should possess this. Search, O search the precious Bible with hungry hearts. Explore God's word... Never give up the search until you have ascertained your relation to God and His will in regard to you. Christ declared, "Whatsoever ye shall ask in My name, that will I do, that the Father may be glorified in the Son. If ye shall ask anything in My name, I will do it" John 14:13, 14 (Christ's Object Lessons, page 111 paragraph 3).

God speaks in His word, and fulfills this word in the world. We need now to seek to understand the movements of God's providence. Said Paul, "Ye, brethren, are not in darkness, that that day should overtake you as a thief. Ye are all the children of light, and the children of the day: we are not of the night nor of darkness." *God's people are not left to depend on man's wisdom.* With prophetic guideposts God has marked out the way He wishes them to take. These great waymarks show us that the path of obedience is the only path we can follow with certainty. Men break their word, and prove themselves untrustworthy, but God changes not. His word will abide the same forever. Those who love and obey the law of Jehovah will meet with trial and temptation; but these are only what Jesus met, and He declares: "My sheep hear My voice, and I know them, and they follow Me: and I give unto them eternal life; and they shall never perish, neither shall any man pluck them out of My hand." If we hope and pray, and by faith trust His word...[nothing] "shall be able to separate us from the love of God, which is in Christ Jesus our Lord" (RH, Feb. 6, 1900, paragraph 11).

God's word is sure! Our understanding of it will increase, as the Holy Spirit continues to impress Present Truth upon our hearts. Bible prophecies confirm that God is all knowing. Our increased understanding of the mysteries that have been hidden in plain sight for centuries will strengthen our faith and trust in our Omniscient all-loving Creator. The apostle Paul refers to "the ministers of Christ" as "stewards of the mysteries of God," and of their work he declares: "It is required in stewards, that a man be found faithful" (cf 1 Corinthians 4:1-5). Jesus promises His faithful followers:

> Unto you it is given to know the mysteries of the kingdom of God: but to others in parables; that seeing they might not see, and hearing they might not understand (Luke 8:10).

As the second appearing of our Lord Jesus Christ draws near, satanic agencies are moved from beneath. *Satan will not only appear as a human being,* but *he will personate Jesus Christ*; and the world who has rejected the truth will receive him as the Lord of lords and King of kings. He will exercise his power, and work upon the human imagination. *He will corrupt both the minds and the bodies of men,* and will work through the children of disobedience, fascinating and charming, as does a serpent. What a spectacle for God, the Creator of the world, to behold! *The form Satan assumed in Eden when leading our first parents to transgress was of a character to bewilder and confuse the mind. He will work in as subtle a manner as we near the end of earth's history. All his deceiving power will be brought to bear upon human subjects, to complete the work of deluding the human family.* So deceptive will be his working, that men will do as they did in the days of Christ... Christ will be represented in the person of those who accept the truth, and who identify their interest with that of their Lord (Review and Herald, April 14, 1896, paragraph 6).

Before personating Christ, *Satan personates a human being.* Who? The beast with seven heads (Revelation 17:9) is the papal beast of 13:1-10. Their heads depict popes: Pius VI was the head that received the deadly wound, and the Pius head was healed thru the Lateran Treaty. The seven post1929 solo popes were: Pius XI & XII, John XXIII, Paul VI, John-Paul I (the five that were fallen), John-Paul II (the one that is), and Benedict XVI (the short space pope; cf Revelation 17:9-10). His abdication changed the papacy from a solo monarchy to a dual monarchy as ancient Babylon had had two kings when it was about to fall. In an instant, ancient Babylon had three kings: Nabonidus, Belshazzar and Daniel, the third ruler, moments before Babylon fell. Revelation 17 explains that "the eighth is of the seven": That cannot be Pope Francis I, who is the eighth chronologically, because he is not *of the seven.* The eighth pope is one of the dead popes. Pope John-Paul II was identified as *the one that is,* and that is not, for he died like *the beast that was, and is not, even he is the eighth, and is of the seven, and goeth into perdition* (17:11). Who goes to perdition, hell's fire?

> *That day shall not come,* except there come a falling away first, and that man of sin be revealed, *the son of perdition;* who opposeth and *exalteth himself above all that is called God,* or that is worshipped; so that *he as God sitteth in the temple of God, shewing himself that he is God* (2 Thessalonians 2:3, 4).

> Take up this proverb against *the king of Babylon,* and say...*Hell from beneath is moved for thee to meet thee at thy coming...O Lucifer...*For thou hast said in thine heart, I will ascend into heaven, *I will exalt my throne* above the stars of God...*I will be like the Most High* (cf Isaiah 14).

Satan, the dragon, receives a deadly wound when he is bound for a thousand years. He is released for a little while, and then he goes to perdition (cf Revelation 20). This *king of Babylon* personates Pope John-Paul II: the one who is and died and thus, appears to live again. End time Spiritual Babylon has two living popes, and it will soon have a third, as per Revelation 16:13: *the dragon* (Satan personating John-Paul II), *the beast* (Francis I), *and the false prophet* (Benedict).

False prophets "deceive many...insomuch that, if it were possible, they shall deceive the very elect" (Matthew 24:11, 24). Are popes "false prophets...false teachers among you, who privily shall *bring in damnable heresies*, even denying the Lord that bought them, and bring upon themselves swift destruction" (2 Peter 2:1)? Pope Francis I urges nations to legalize civil unions in spite of the Roman Church's CONGREGATION FOR THE DOCTRINE OF THE FAITH condemning: "the immoral nature of these unions" as sin!

> *Are not such teachers the pretenders to whom Christ referred when He said, "Beware of false prophets*, which come to you..." in opposition to the requirements of God ...*the pope of Rome...* claims great spiritual riches...and boasts of the grace of Christ, which he has turned into *lasciviousness...* (RH, July 24, 1888, paragraph 11).

> In the last days Satan will appear as an angel of light, with great power and heavenly glory, and claim to be the Lord of the whole earth. He will declare that the Sabbath has been changed from the seventh to the first day of the week; and as lord of the first day of the week he will present this spurious sabbath as a test of loyalty to him. Then will take place the final fulfillment of the Revelator's prophecy (19MR 282.1).

When Satan personates Pope John-Paul II, the man who declared that God made Sunday the Sabbath in Dies Domini, clearly, he cannot be this dead pope. His body is in a Vatican crypt. Those who do not know the Bible teaching that the dead are dead will be deceived. "*The soul that sinneth, it shall die*" (Ezekiel 18:20). "For the living know that they shall die: but the dead know not anything" (Ecclesiastes 9:5). "[As] the cloud...vanisheth away: so, he that goeth down to the grave shall come up no [more]. *He shall return no more to his house, neither shall his place know him anymore*" (Job 7:9-10).

Spiritualism is about to take the world captive... Superhuman power is working... The foundation for the success of Spiritualism...ministers have proclaimed, as Bible doctrines, falsehoods...consciousness after death, of the spirits of the dead being in communion with the living...[with] no foundation in the Scriptures, and yet this theory is affirmed as truth. Through this false doctrine the way has been opened for *the spirits of devils* to deceive the people in *representing themselves as the dead.* Satanic agencies personate the dead, and thus bring souls into captivity...*he uses all manner of deception* (ST, May 28, 1894, paragraph 3).

Through the two great errors, the immortality of the soul, and Sunday sacredness, Satan will bring the people under his deceptions. While the former lays the foundation of Spiritualism, the latter creates a bond of sympathy with Rome. The Protestants of the United States will be foremost in stretching their hands across the gulf to grasp the hand of Spiritualism; they will reach over the abyss to clasp hands with the Roman power; and under the influence of this threefold union, this country [USA] will follow in the steps of Rome in trampling on the rights of conscience (GC88 588.1).

Jesus had left it.--Satan appeared to be by the throne ...I saw them look up to the throne and pray, my Father give us Thy Spirit; then *Satan would breathe upon them an unholy influence; in it there was light and much power, but no sweet love, joy and peace.* Satan's object was to keep them deceived, and to draw back and deceive God's children. I saw one after another leave the company who were praying to Jesus in the Holiest...and join those before the throne, and they at once received the unholy influence of Satan (Broadside1, April 6, 1846 par. 7).

Trouble Ahead

And the beast which I saw was like unto a leopard, and his feet were as *[the feet]* of a bear, and his mouth as the mouth of a lion: and *the dragon gave him his power, and his seat, and great authority* (Revelation 13:2).

As it was in the days of Noah, it will be in the end time. When God's judgment was about to fall on *Noah's* world, he knew when to go into the ark; he entered, and waited 7 days. After the Judgment Hour allotted for the living ended on February 14, 2013, a seven-day wait (each day being a year), ended February 14, 2020. What then? That very day, a bomb cyclone formed that struck Iceland, England, and Europe and the World Health Organization declared COVID19 a global pandemic. It is a judgment from God just as sure as the flood in Noah's day! Do the waymarks foretell the final seven-years? The Mark of the Beast is about to be revealed!

The 3rd angel followed them, *saying with a loud voice, If any man worship the beast and his image, and receive his mark in his forehead, or in his hand,* the same shall drink of the wine of the wrath of God, which is poured out without mixture into the cup of His indignation; and he shall be tormented with fire and brimstone in the presence of the holy angels, and in the presence of the Lamb: And the smoke of their torment ascendeth up for ever and ever: and they have no rest day nor night, who worship the beast and his image, and whosoever receiveth the mark of his name. *Here is the patience of the saints: here are they that keep the commandments of God, and the faith of Jesus* (Revelation 14:9-12).

The decree is to go forth that *all who will not receive the mark of the beast shall neither buy nor sell* and finally that they shall be put to death (ST, Nov. 8, 1899 par. 11).

*Christendom will be divided into two great classes,—
those who keep the commandments of God and the faith
of Jesus, and those who worship the beast and his image
and receive his mark. Although church and State will
unite their power to compel 'all, both small and great, rich
and poor, free and bond,' to receive 'the mark of the beast,'
[Revelation 13:16.] yet the people of God will not receive it*
(GC88 450.1).

In addition to the Ten Commandments, God gives other
commands in the Bible. "Command thou the people, saying
...Ye shall buy" (Deuteronomy 2:4, 6). "The command must
be obeyed, 'Sell that ye have...'" (Luke 12:33) {8MR 206.2}.

Those who, after the light regarding God's law comes
to them, continue to disobey, and exalt human laws
above the law of God in the great crisis before us, will
receive the mark of the beast (KC 148.4).

If we receive this mark *in our foreheads or in our
hands*, the judgments pronounced against the
disobedient must fall upon us (RH, April 27, 1911 par. 26).

By this first beast is represented the Roman Church
...The image to the beast represents another religious
body...the United States. Here is to be found an image of
the Papacy. When the churches of our land, uniting
upon such points of faith as are held by them in common,
shall influence the State to enforce their decrees and
sustain their institutions, then will Protestant America
have formed an image of the Roman hierarchy. Then the
true church will be assailed by persecution, as were
God's ancient people (SR 381.2).

*The beast with lamblike horns commands "all, both
small and great, rich and poor, free and bond, to receive a
mark in their right hand, or in their foreheads: and that no
man might buy or sell, save he that had the mark, or the*

name of the beast, or the number of his name" Revelation *13:16, 17. This is the mark concerning which the third angel utters his warning.* It is the mark of the first beast, or the Papacy, and is therefore to be...among the distinguishing characteristics of that power (SR 382.1).

The light that we have upon the third angel's message is the true light. The mark of the beast is exactly what it has been proclaimed to be. Not all in regard to this matter is yet understood, and will not be understood until the unrolling of the scroll; but a most solemn work is to be accomplished in our world. The Lord's command to His servants is: 'Cry aloud, spare not, lift up thy voice like a trumpet, and show My people their transgression, and the house of Jacob their sins.' [Isaiah 58:1] A message that will arouse the churches is to be proclaimed. Every effort is to be made to give the light, not only to our people, but to the world... *The prophecies of Daniel and the Revelation...with the necessary explanations...should be sent all over the world. Our own people need to have the light placed before them in clearer lines* (Testimonies Vol. 8, page 159 paragraph 3).

Not all who profess to keep the Sabbath will be sealed. There are many even among those who teach the truth to others who will not receive the seal of God in their foreheads. They had the light of truth, they knew their Master's will, they understood every point of our faith, but they had not corresponding works. These who were so familiar with prophecy and the treasures of divine wisdom, should have acted their faith. They should have commanded their households after them, that by a well-ordered family they might present to the world the influence of the truth upon the human heart (Christian Experiences and Teachings, p. 189 par. 1).

The Spirit of God is gradually but surely being withdrawn from the earth. Plagues and judgments are already falling upon the despisers of the grace of God. The calamities by land and sea, the unsettled state of society, the alarms of war, are portentous. They forecast approaching events of the greatest magnitude. The agencies of evil are combining their forces, and consolidating. They are strengthening for the last great crisis. *Great changes are soon to take place in our world, and the final movements will be rapid ones* (9T 11.1-2).

We have only a little while to urge the warfare; then Christ will come, and this scene of rebellion will close. Then our last efforts will have been made to work with Christ and advance His kingdom. Some who have stood in the forefront of the battle, zealously resisting incoming evil, fall at the post of duty; others gaze sorrowfully at the fallen heroes, but have no time to cease work. They must close up the ranks, seize the banner from the hand palsied by death, and with renewed energy vindicate the truth and the honor of Christ. As never before, resistance must be made against sin,--against the powers of darkness. The time demands energetic and determined activity on the part of those who believe present truth. They should teach the truth by both precept and example. If the time seems long to wait for our Deliverer to come, if, bowed by affliction and worn with toil, we feel impatient for our commission to close, and to receive an honorable release from the warfare, let us remember-and let the remembrance check every murmur--that God leaves us on earth to encounter storms and conflicts, to perfect Christian character, to become better acquainted with God our Father and Christ our elder Brother, and to do work for the Master in winning many souls to Christ, that with glad heart we may hear the words: "Well done, good and faithful servant; enter thou into the joy of thy Lord" (RH, October 25, 1881, par. 10).

Daniel 12. Read attentively this chapter. "*Hear the word of the LORD, ye children of Israel: for the LORD hath a controversy with the inhabitants of the land, because [there is] no truth, nor mercy, nor knowledge of God in the land.* By swearing, and lying, and killing, and stealing, and committing adultery, they break out, and blood toucheth blood. Therefore, shall the land mourn, and every one that dwelleth therein shall languish, with the beasts of the field, and with the fowls of heaven; yea, the fishes of the sea also shall be taken away. Yet let no man strive, nor reprove another: for thy people [are] as they that strive with the priest. *Therefore, shalt thou fall in the day, and the prophet also shall fall with thee in the night, and I will destroy thy mother. My people are destroyed for lack of knowledge: because thou hast rejected knowledge, I will also reject thee, that thou shalt be no priest to me: seeing thou hast forgotten the law of thy God, I will also forget thy children"* Hosea 4:1-6 (18MR 220.4).

The great burden of every soul should be, Is my heart renewed? Is my soul transformed? Are my sins pardoned through faith in Christ? Have I been born again? Am I complying with the invitation, "Come unto me, all ye that labor and are heavy laden, and I will give you rest. Take My yoke upon you, and learn of Me; for I am meek and lowly in heart: and ye shall find rest unto your souls. For My yoke is easy, and My burden is light" [Matthew 11:28]. Do you count all things but loss for the excellency of the knowledge of Christ Jesus? And do you feel it your duty to believe every word that proceeds out of the mouth of God? (17MR 23.3).

The unprepared condition of our churches...The Lord showed...[Paul] many things that it is not lawful for a man to utter. Why could he not tell the believers what he had seen? Because *they would have made a misapplication of the great truths presented.* They would not have been able to comprehend these truths...[that] God gave him to bear to the churches (15MR 228.1).

The people of God need to study what characters they must form in order to pass through the test and proving of the last days. Many are living in spiritual weakness and backsliding. They know not what they believe. Let us read and study the twelfth chapter of Daniel. It is a warning that we shall all need to understand before the time of the end. There are ministers claiming to believe the truth who are not sanctified through the truth (15MR 228.2).

We must know for ourselves that the Spirit of God is abiding in our hearts, and that we can hold communion with God. Then if He should come to us quickly, if by any chance our life should suddenly be ended, we should be ready to meet our God. Now, while it is called today, let us set our house in order. "Today if ye will hear His voice, harden not your hearts as in the provocation." Because of their unbelief of God's Word, the children of Israel who left Egypt perished in the wilderness. God grant that we may not through unbelief fail of entering into the Promised Land. Let us keep step with Jesus Christ (GCB, April 6, 1903 par. 2).

The signs of the times are fulfilling in our world, yet the churches generally are represented as slumbering. Shall we not take warning from the experience of the foolish virgins, who when the call came, "Behold the bridegroom cometh; go ye out to meet him," found that they had no oil in their lamps? And while they went to buy oil, the bridegroom went in to the marriage supper with the wise virgins, and the door was shut. When the foolish virgins reached the banqueting hall, they received an unexpected denial. The master of the feast declared, "I know you not." They were left standing without in the empty street, in the blackness of the night (15MR 229.1).

Now, while our great High Priest is making the atonement for us, we should seek to become perfect in Christ. Not even by a thought could our Saviour be brought to yield to the power of temptation. Satan finds in human hearts some point where he can gain a foothold; some sinful desire is cherished, by means of which his temptations assert their power. But Christ declared of Himself, "The prince of this world cometh, and hath nothing in Me." Satan could find nothing in the Son of God that would enable him to gain the victory. He had kept His Father's commandments, and there was no sin in Him that Satan could use to his advantage. This is the condition in which those must be found who shall stand in the time of trouble (RH, March 14, 1912 par. 8).

Remember that you will never reach a higher standard than you yourselves set. Set your mark high, and then step by step, even though it be by painful effort, by self-denial and self-sacrifice, ascend the whole length of the ladder of progress. Let nothing hinder you. Christ will be to you a present help in every time of trouble. Stand like Daniel, the faithful statesman, a man whom no temptation could corrupt... *Do not disappoint Him who so loved you that He gave His own life to cancel your sins.* He says: "Without Me ye can do nothing." *Remember this, If you have made mistakes, you certainly gain a victory if you see these mistakes, and regard them as beacons of warning.* I need not tell you that thus you turn defeat into victory, disappointing the enemy and honoring your Redeemer (1NL 81.5).

Notice our place in prophetic history. The seven headed papacy has yielded to the earth-beast, USA. Its *duo* (fourth) horn/President is in office in the midst of the COVID-19 plague. In the war against COVID, America is urging the masses to take a vaccine based on new technology that it promises to be a panacea against severe COVID illness and death. The Mark of the Beast is pending as are the seven last plagues. Notice that the first plague is a sore that will not heal that comes immediately after the Mark of the Beast.

The timing: A powerful angel has lightened the earth with his glory. Fallen Babylon is identified by its fornication. People flowing into the Roman Church is waning. Her sins reached heaven when the Judgment Hour ended February 14, 2013. Her punishment is about to be dispensed. Flee from Babylon to avoid her judgments and her plagues. Pope Francis I's light show demonstrated that Babylon is a cage of unclean birds. The majority Catholic US Supreme Court has codified the wine of Babylon's fornication into law. The earth-king, President Obama, praised their rebellion against God's word as a victory. The Mark of the Beast and the seven last plagues await their appointed time: The first plague is a sore that will not heal. Please tell, what is that painful sore that is to afflict folks in the end time? Where does it come from? Should we imagine that it does not link to COVID-19?

The things of this world are about to close... See the waymarks that are all along the way. When we are traveling...and see a guide board; *if we can read, we know that we are at such a place; so, it is if our minds are active and so consecrated to God that we can understand His workings, we can know just where we are in this world's history...* The powers of darkness are working with an intensity from within, but God has been working for us, and He will work for us that Christ shall not have died in vain, that we may have of the life that runs parallel with the life of Jehovah. It is this little, little atom of a world that is absorbing all our force (2SAT 48.5).

And I heard a great voice out of the temple saying to the seven angels, Go your ways, and *pour out the vials of the wrath of God* [seven last plagues] upon the earth. And the first went, and poured out his vial upon the earth; *and there fell a noisome and grievous sore upon the men which had the mark of the beast, and* upon *them which worshipped his image* (Revelation 16:1-2).

Satan *is launching* the Time of Trouble. Are you ready?

The Jab

Jesus warned, "How dreadful it will be in those days for pregnant women and nursing mothers!" (Matthew 24:19, NIV). Why did Jesus give this warning? What is He teaching us in the end time? Has that time past? If not, when?

Retirement funds, 401K's and financial planning to have a secure future seem reasonable. But will there be a time that our possessions will curse us? How will having a house mortgage, car payments, unpaid debts, or a large amount of money in the bank impact our life when the Mark of the Beast is implemented? Will we hear Christ's, "Well done good and faithful servant?" Or will God view us as the selfish rich man?

> The ground of a certain rich man brought forth plentifully: And he thought within himself, saying, What shall I do, because I have no room where to bestow my fruits? And he said, This will I do: I will pull down my barns, and build greater; and there will I bestow all my fruits and my goods. And I will say to my soul, Soul, thou hast much goods laid up for many years; take thine ease, eat, drink, *and* be merry. But God said unto him, *Thou* fool, this night thy soul shall be required of thee: then whose shall those things be, which thou hast provided? So. *is* he that layeth up treasure for himself, and is not rich toward God (Luke 12:16-21).

> Your gold and silver...shall be a witness against you, and shall eat your flesh as it were fire. Ye have heaped treasure together for the last days (James 5:3).

How do we know when it is time to give our offerings to the LORD to finish His work as Israel gave in the wilderness? Instead of having our possessions consume our flesh, it would be better to use them for God like the poor widow.

> This poor widow hath cast more in, than all they which have cast into the treasury: For all *they* did cast in

of their abundance; but she of her want did cast in all that she had, *even* all her living (Matthew 12:42-43).

Jesus forewarns us of pending danger because He wants us to understand and to prepare for the coming conflict. With the dreaded 666 *Mark of the beast* coming, it will be dangerous to be in the military. After the Mark of the Beast is in place, being in the armed services will not merely be *having a secure government job.* It will be a curse! Do not wait and see! It is time to heed the Third Angel's Message.

In Revelation 13 this subject is plainly presented: "I beheld *another beast coming up out of the earth*; and he had two *horns like a lamb*, and he *spake as a dragon.* And he exercised all the power of the first beast before him, and causeth the earth and them that dwell therein to worship the first beast, whose deadly wound was healed." *Then the miracle-working power is revealed:* "And *deceiveth them that dwell on the earth by the means of those miracles which he had power to do in the sight of the beast*; saying to them that dwell on the earth, that they should make an image to the beast, which had the wound by a sword, and did live. And he had power to give life unto the image of the beast, that the image of the beast should both speak, and cause that as many as would not worship the image of the beast should be killed. *And he causeth all, both small and great, rich and poor, free and bond, to receive a mark in their right hand, or in their foreheads and that no man might buy or sell, save he that had the mark, or the name of the beast, or the number of his name*" (1888 700.2).

Revelation is a sealed book, but it is also an open book, recording marvelous events that are to take place in the last days of this earth's history. *Its teachings are definite, not mystical and unintelligible, and God would have us understand it* (ST, January 11, 1899 par. 5).

It was *through putting a mystical meaning upon the plain words of God, that sacred and vital truths were made of little significance, while the theories of men were made prominent.* It was in this way that men were led to teach for doctrines the commandments of men, and that they rejected the commandment of God, that they might keep their own tradition (RH June 2, 1896, par. 7).

In every place God is working to bring us to a knowledge of Christ and His righteousness. He speaks to us in His Word. The Bible is the key that unlocks the mysteries which it is essential for us to understand in order to know what we must do to gain eternal life. The Bible is its own expositor. Its bright beams are to shine into all parts of the world, that sin may be revealed. The Bible is a chart, pointing out the waymarks of truth. Those who are acquainted with this chart will be enabled to tread with certainty the path of duty, wherever we may be called to go (7MR 236.2).

The truth should have been proclaimed by the ten virgins, but only five had made the provision essential to join that company who walked in the light that had come to them. *The third angel's message was needed. This proclamation was to be made. Many who went forth to meet the Bridegroom under the messages of the first and second angels, refused the third angel's message, the last testing message to be given to the world* (16MR 269.3).

The Lord is testing His people to see who will be loyal to the principles of His truth. *Our work is to proclaim to the world the first, second, and third angels' messages.* In the discharge of our duties, we are neither to despise nor to fear our enemies... We are to treat with kindness and courtesy those who refuse to be loyal to God, but we are never, never to unite with them in counsel regarding the vital interests of His work. Putting our trust in God, we are to move steadily forward, doing His work with unselfishness, in humble dependence upon Him, committing to His providence ourselves and all that concerns our present and future, holding the beginning of our confidence firm unto the end, remembering that we receive the blessings of heaven, not because of our worthiness, but because of Christ's worthiness and our acceptance, through faith in Him, of God's abounding grace (7T 107.2).

Unions are one of the signs of the last days. Men are binding up in bundles ready to be burned. They may be church members, but while they belong to these unions, they cannot possibly keep the commandments of God; for to belong to these unions means to disregard the entire decalogue (4MR 75.4).

"Thou shalt love the Lord thy God with all thy heart, and with all thy soul, and with all thy strength, and with all thy mind; and thy neighbor as thyself," (Luke 10:27). These words sum up the whole duty of man. They mean the consecration of the whole being, body, soul, and spirit, to God's service. How can men obey these words, and at the same time pledge themselves to support that which deprives their neighbors of freedom of action? And how can men obey these words, and form combinations that rob the poorer classes of the advantages which justly belong to them, preventing them from buying or selling, except under certain conditions! How plainly the words of God have predicted this condition of things. John writes, "I beheld another beast coming up out of the earth; and he had two horns like a lamb, and he spake as a dragon. . . . And he causeth all, both small and great, rich and poor, free and bond, to receive a mark in their right hand, or in the foreheads: and that no man might buy or sell, save he that had the mark, or the name of the beast, or the number of his name" (4MR 75.5).

The Forming of These Unions Is One of Satan's Last Efforts. God calls upon people to get out of the cities, isolating themselves from the world. The time will come when they will have to do this. *God will care for those who love Him and keep His commandments* (4MR 76.1).

We must now put on the whole armor of righteousness. We must be as true as steel to principle, standing steadfastly against every species of corruption. It is this steadfast adherence to principle that is to distinguish those who bear the seal of the living God from those who have the mark of the beast (4MR 76.2).

The Third Angel's Message is the test that will separate those who have the seal of God from those who have the 666 Mark of the Beast. As God has warned us in Revelation not to take the Mark of the Beast, He warns us thru Ellen G. White that union membership will have a part to play in last day events. But that is not the entire end time message.

Have you noticed that the fear of COVID-19 has led many to call for a universal vaccination passport? Is it different than schools requiring shot records for students? The Biden administration is resisting nationwide vaccination passports, and the governors of Florida and Texas have banned them because of concerns about *ethical issues, discrimination, inequality, privacy and fraud.* But Israel requires vaccination passports for travel and for attendance at group events. Peer pressure is covertly being applied to everyone to take the jab *for their own safety and to keep others safe.* Due to the timing of the issue, it is a forerunner of the Mark of the Beast: The law of the land that precedes the seven last plagues.

The first plague is a sore that will not heal. Who gets this painful sore? Those who have the Mark! What disease causes this plague? The Bible does not say. It states that this end time sore will afflict those who have the Beast's Mark!

Know where we are in Bible prophecy! Babylon is fallen because of her fornication! The Mark is the next waymark!

Did you realize that since a few folks have had rare blood clots linked to the more traditional vaccines that the masses are predominantly getting the experimental mRNA COVID-19 jab? Is it wise to presume that it is safe? Do the scientists, doctors, politicians, and the promotional ad campaigns know more than God? The LORD is able to keep His people from COVID, but He may allow us to die. "Many will be laid away to sleep before the fiery ordeal of the time of trouble shall come upon our world" (CH 375.2). "Many little ones are to be laid away before the time of trouble" (CG 566.1). Is the fear of dying from COVID-19 and the desire to live motivating people to take the mRNA jab that might be the cause of the painful sore: The plague that our all-wise God would keep us from? Will God's people perish for lack of knowledge?

It is not always safe to ask for unconditional healing. Let your prayer include this thought: "Lord, You know every secret of the soul. You are acquainted with these persons; for Jesus, their Advocate, gave His life for them. He loves them better than we possibly can. If, therefore it is for Your glory, and the good of these afflicted ones to raise them up to health, we ask in the name of Jesus, that health may be given them at this time." In a petition of this kind no lack of faith is manifested. There are cases that are clear, and the Lord works with His divine power decidedly, in their restoration. The will of God is evidence too plainly to be misunderstood (GCDB, February 26, 1897 par. 5, *language updated*).

The Lord "doth not afflict willingly nor grieve the children of men." "Like as a father pitieth his children, so the Lord pitieth them that fear Him; for He knoweth our frame: He remembereth that we are dust." He knows our heart, for He reads every secret of the soul. *He knows whether or not those...would be able to endure the trial and test that would come upon them if they lived. He knows the end from the beginning. Many will be laid away to sleep in Jesus before the fiery ordeal of the time of trouble shall come upon our world.* This is another reason why we should say after our earnest petition: "Nevertheless not my will, but thine, O Lord, be done." Such a petition will never be registered in heaven as a faithless prayer (GCDB, February 26, 1897 par. 6).

Faith vs presumption: Presuming that taking this jab to save one's life is the will of God is presumption! If God's will is to lay us to rest to preserve us through the Time of Trouble, superimposing our will above that of God will hurt us. Yes, God wants us to prosper and have good health, and He gives us medical knowledge to do just that. But there are people that physically cannot endure the Time of Trouble. God knows if it is best for them to rest in our graves until it is over! If Christians do not understand the issues concerning the Mark of the Beast; they may compel themselves to endure the Time of Trouble that God would spare them from. Rather than putting their house in order, these folks seek to prolong their lives. Thus, they may face trials that will eternally doom them. What if these vaccinated Christians develop a sore that will not heal, like the Israelites faced the first plague in ancient Egypt? Is it just a side effect of the jab, or evidence that they have received the Mark of the Beast? Imagine the doubts and fears and the anguish that will torment them.

Obedience to the word of God is a matter of life or death. It is not optional! When the last plagues fall, they will fall upon Babylon and the people who remain in Babylon. But God's faithful people will be saved when the seven final plagues fall. Our eternal life depends upon our hearing and obeying God's call to flee Babylon. "You shall know the truth and the truth shall set you free." COVID shut down activities that have absorbed our interests and distracted us from God!

There are thousands upon thousands, millions upon millions, who are now making their decision for eternal life or eternal death. The man who is wholly absorbed in his counting room, the man who finds pleasure at the gaming table, the man who loves to indulge perverted appetite, the amusement lover, the frequenters of the theater [TV] and the ballroom, put eternity out of their reckoning. The whole burden of their life is: What shall we eat? what shall we drink? And wherewithal shall we be clothed? They are not in the procession that is moving heavenward. They are led by the great apostate, and with him will be destroyed (6T 406.7, *supplemented*).

Unless we understand the importance of the moments that are swiftly passing into eternity, and make ready to stand in the great day of God, we shall be unfaithful stewards. *The watchman is to know the time of night.* Everything is now clothed with a solemnity that all who believe the truth for this time should realize. They should act in reference to the day of God. The judgments of God are about to fall upon the world, and we need to be preparing for that great day (6T 407.1).

Our time is precious. We have but few, very few days of probation in which to make ready for the future, immortal life. We have no time to spend in haphazard movements. We should fear to skim the surface of the word of God (6T 407.2).

It is as true now as when Christ was upon the earth, that every inroad made by the gospel upon the enemy's dominion is met by fierce opposition from his vast armies. *The conflict that is right upon us will be the most terrible ever witnessed.* But though Satan is represented as being as strong as the strong man armed, his overthrow will be complete, and everyone who unites with him in choosing apostasy rather than loyalty will perish with him (6T 407.3).

The Last Plagues

The Saviour's prophecy concerning the visitation of judgments upon Jerusalem is to have another fulfillment, of which that terrible desolation was but a faint shadow. In the fate of the chosen city, we may behold the doom of a world that has rejected God's mercy and trampled upon His law (GC 36.2).

Many have unsubdued, unhumbled hearts, and think more of their own little grievances and trials than of the souls of sinners. If they had the glory of God in view, they would feel for perishing souls around them; and as they realized their perilous situation, would take hold with energy, exercising faith in God, and hold up the hands of His servants, that they might boldly, yet in love, declare the truth and warn souls to lay hold upon it before the sweet voice of mercy should die away. Said the angel, "Those who profess His name are not ready." I saw that the seven last plagues were coming upon the shelterless heads of the wicked; and then those who have stood in their way will hear the bitter reproaches of sinners, and their hearts will faint within them (Early Writings, page 120 paragraph 3).

I saw that the mysterious signs and wonders and false reformations would increase and spread. The reformations that were shown me were not reformations from error to truth... (EW 45.1).

Satan was trying...to hold them where they were, until the sealing was past, until the covering was drawn over God's people, and they left without a shelter from the burning wrath of God, in the seven last plagues. God has begun to draw this covering over His people, and it will soon be drawn over all who are to have a shelter in the day of slaughter. God will work in power for His people; and Satan will be permitted to work... (EW 44.2).

Here is a channel wholly devoted to himself and under his control, and he can make the world believe what he will. The Book that is to judge him and his followers he puts back in the shade, just where he wants it. The Saviour of the world he makes to be no more than a common man...the poor, deluded followers of these pretended spiritual manifestations repeat and try to make it appear that there is nothing miraculous about our Saviour's birth, death, and resurrection. After putting Jesus in the background, they attract the attention of the world to themselves and to their miracles and lying wonders, which, they declare, far exceed the works of Christ. Thus, the world is taken in the snare and lulled into a feeling of security, not to find out their awful deception until the seven last plagues are poured out. Satan laughs as he sees his plan succeed so well and the whole world taken in the snare (EW 91.2).

Jesus would not leave the most holy place until every case was decided either for salvation or destruction, and that the wrath of God could not come until Jesus had finished His work in the Most Holy place, laid off His priestly attire, and clothed Himself with the garments of vengeance. Then Jesus will step out from between the Father and man, and God will keep silence no longer, but pour out His wrath on those who have rejected His truth. I saw that the anger of the nations, the wrath of God, and the time to judge the dead were separate and distinct, one following the other, also that Michael had not stood up, and that the time of trouble, such as never was, had not yet commenced. The nations are now getting angry, but when our High Priest has finished His work in the sanctuary, He will stand up, put on the garments of vengeance, and then the seven last plagues will be poured out (EW 36.1).

These plagues enraged the wicked against the righteous; they thought that we had brought the judgments of God upon them, and that if they could rid the earth of us, the plagues would then be stayed. A decree went forth to slay the saints, which caused them to cry day and night for deliverance. This was the time of Jacob's trouble. Then all the saints cried out with anguish of spirit, and were delivered by the voice of God. The 144,000 triumphed. Their faces were lighted up with the glory of God. Then I was shown a company who were howling in agony. On their garments was written in large characters, "Thou art weighed in the balance, and found wanting." I asked who this company were. The angel said, "These are they who have once kept the Sabbath and have given it up." I heard them cry with a loud voice, "We have believed in Thy coming, and taught it with energy." And while they were speaking, their eyes would ...see the writing, and then they would wail aloud. I saw that they had drunk of the deep waters, and fouled the residue with their feet--trodden the Sabbath underfoot-- and that was why they were...found wanting (EW 36.2).

The seven last plagues were soon to be poured out upon those who have no shelter; yet the world regarded them no more than they would so many drops of water that were about to fall. I was then made capable of enduring the awful sight of the seven last plagues, the wrath of God. I saw that His anger was dreadful and terrible, and if He should stretch forth His hand, or lift it in anger, the inhabitants of the world would be as though they had never been, or *would suffer from incurable sores and withering plagues that would come upon them*, and they would find no deliverance, but be destroyed by them. Terror seized me, and...I realized, as never before, the importance of searching the Word of God carefully, to *know how to escape the plagues which that Word declares shall come on all the ungodly who shall worship the beast and his image and receive his mark in their foreheads or in their hands.* It was a great wonder for me that any could transgress the law of God and tread down His holy Sabbath, when such awful threatenings and denunciations were against them (EW 64.2).

The pope has changed the day of rest from the seventh to the first day. He has thought to change the very commandment that was given to cause man to remember his Creator. He has thought to change the greatest commandment in the decalogue and thus make himself equal with God, or even exalt himself above God. *The Lord is unchangeable; therefore, His law is immutable; but the pope has exalted himself above God, in seeking to change His immutable precepts of holiness, justice, and goodness. He has trampled underfoot God's sanctified day, and, on his own authority, put in its place one of the six laboring days.* The whole nation has followed after the beast, and every week they rob God of His holy time. The pope has made a breach in the holy law of God, but ... the time had fully come for this breach to be made up by the people of God... (EW 65.1).

At that time the "latter rain," or refreshing from the presence of the Lord, will come, to give power to the loud voice of the third angel, and prepare the saints to stand in the period when the seven last plagues shall be poured out (EW 86.1).

When the plagues begin to fall, those who continue to break the holy Sabbath will not open their mouths to plead those excuses that they now make to get rid of keeping it. Their mouths will be closed while the plagues are falling, and the great Lawgiver is requiring justice of those who have had His holy law in derision and have called it "a curse to man," "miserable," and "rickety." When such feel the iron grasp of this law taking hold of them, these expressions will appear before them in living characters, and they will then realize the sin of having that law in derision which the Word of God calls "holy, just, and good" (EW 65.2).

The plagues were falling upon the inhabitants of the earth. Some were denouncing God and cursing Him. Others rushed to the people of God and begged to be taught how they might escape His judgments. But the saints had nothing for them. The last tear for sinners had been shed, the last agonizing prayer offered, the last burden borne, the last warning given (EW 281.1).

When Christ ceases His intercession in the sanctuary, the unmingled wrath threatened against those who worship the beast and his image and receive his mark (Revelation 14:9, 10), will be poured out. The plagues upon Egypt when God was about to deliver Israel, were similar in character to those more terrible and extensive judgments which are to fall upon the world just before the final deliverance of God's people. Says the revelator, in describing those terrific scourges: "There fell a noisome and grievous sore upon the men which had the mark of the beast, and upon them which worshiped his image." The sea "became as the blood of a dead man: And every living soul died in the sea" (GC 627.3).

Is it possible that the universal mRNA COVID-19 jab will cause the first plague? Could the plague on the sea link to an oilwell disaster like the Deepwater Horizon or a seaquake?

"The rivers and fountains of waters . . . became blood." Terrible as these inflictions are, God's justice stands fully vindicated. The angel of God declares: "Thou art righteous, O Lord, . . . because Thou hast judged thus. For they have shed the blood of saints and prophets, and Thou hast given them blood to drink; for they are worthy." Rev 16:2-6. By condemning the people of God to death, they have as truly incurred the guilt of their blood as if it had been shed by their hands... They possessed the same spirit and were seeking to do the same work with these murderers of the prophets (Ibid.)

In the plague that follows, power is given to the sun "to scorch men with fire. And men were scorched with great heat." Verses 8, 9. The prophets thus describe the condition of the earth at this fearful time: "The land mourns; . . . because the harvest of the field is perished. . . . All the trees of the field are withered: because joy is withered away from the sons of men." "The seed is rotten under their clods; the garners are laid desolate. . . . How do the beasts groan! The herds of cattle are perplexed, because they have no pasture. . . . The rivers of water are dried up, and the fire hath devoured the pastures of the wilderness." "The songs of the temple shall be howlings in that day, saith the Lord God: there shall be many dead bodies in every place; they shall cast them forth with silence." Joel 1:10-12, 17-20; Amos 8:3 (GC 628.1).

Imagine: Plague on the rivers linked to global warming, subterranean aquafers damaged by fracking, and ozone layer depletion making the sun scorch men! Harvesting what we sowed. Armageddon is almost here (cf 6T 406.3).

It cannot now be said by the Lord's servants, as it was by the prophet Daniel: "The time appointed was long." Daniel 10:1. It is now but a short time till the witnesses for God will have done their work in preparing the way of the Lord (6T 406.4).

We are to throw aside our narrow, selfish plans, remembering that we have a work of the largest magnitude and highest importance. In doing this work we are sounding the first, second, and third angels' messages, and are thus being prepared for the coming of that other angel from heaven who is to lighten the earth with his glory (6T 406.5).

We need to study the pouring out of the seventh vial. The powers of evil will not yield up the conflict without a struggle. But Providence has a part to act in the battle of Armageddon. When the earth is lighted with the glory of the angel of Revelation 18, the religious elements, good and evil, will awake from slumber, and the armies of the living God will take the field (19MR 160.1).

Plagues are not universal... Yet *they will be the most awful scourges that have ever been known to mortals.* All the judgments upon men, prior to the close of probation, have been mingled with mercy. The pleading blood of Christ has shielded the sinner from receiving the full measure of his guilt; but in the final judgment, wrath is poured out unmixed with mercy (GC 628.2).

In that day, multitudes will desire the shelter of God's mercy which they have so long despised. "Behold, the days come, saith the Lord God, that I will send a famine in the land, not a famine of bread, nor a thirst for water, but of hearing the words of the Lord: and they shall wander from sea to sea, and from the north even to the east, they shall run to and fro to seek the word of the Lord, and shall not find it." Amos 8:11, 12 (GC 629.1).

The people of God will not be free from suffering; but while persecuted and distressed, while they endure privation and suffer for want of food they will not be left to perish. That God who cared for Elijah will not pass by one of His self-sacrificing children. He who numbers the hairs of their head will care for them, and in time of famine they shall be satisfied. While the wicked are dying from hunger and pestilence, angels will shield the righteous and supply their wants. To him that "walketh righteously" is the promise: "Bread shall be given him; his waters shall be sure." "When the poor and needy seek water, and there is none, and their tongue fails for thirst, I the Lord will hear them, I the God of Israel will not forsake them" Isaiah 33:15, 16; 41:17 (GC 629.2).

With shouts of triumph, jeering, and imprecation, throngs of evil men are about to rush upon their prey, when, lo, a dense blackness, deeper than the darkness of the night, falls upon the earth. Then a rainbow, shining with the glory from the throne of God, spans the heavens and seems to encircle each praying company. The angry multitudes are suddenly arrested. Their mocking cries die away. The objects of their murderous rage are forgotten. With fearful forebodings they gaze upon the symbol of God's covenant and long to be shielded from its overpowering brightness (GC 635.3).

It is at midnight that God manifests His power for the deliverance of His people. The sun appears, shining in its strength. Signs and wonders follow in quick succession. The wicked look with terror and amazement upon the scene, while the righteous behold with solemn joy the tokens of their deliverance... The voice of God like the sound of many waters, saying: "It is done." (GC 636.2).

The whole earth heaves and swells like the waves of the sea. Its surface is breaking up. Its very foundations seem to be giving way. Mountain chains are sinking. Inhabited islands disappear. The seaports that have become like Sodom for wickedness are swallowed up by the angry waters. Babylon the great has come in remembrance before God, "to give unto her the cup of the wine of the fierceness of His wrath." Great hailstones, everyone "about the weight of a talent," are doing their work of destruction. Verses 19, 21... Prison walls are rent asunder, and God's people, who have been held in bondage for their faith, are set free (GC 636.3).

The Conclusion

The restraining Spirit of God is even now being withdrawn from the world. Hurricanes, storms, tempests, fire and flood, disasters by sea and land, follow each other in quick succession. Science seeks to explain all these. The signs thickening around us, telling of the near approach of the Son of God, are attributed to any other than the true cause. Men cannot discern the sentinel angels restraining the four winds that they shall not blow until the servants of God are sealed; but when God shall bid His angels loose the winds, there will be such a scene of strife as no pen can picture (6T 408.1).

To those who are indifferent at this time Christ's warning is: "Because thou art lukewarm, and neither cold nor hot, I will spew thee out of My mouth." Revelation 3:16. The figure of spewing out of His mouth means that He cannot offer- up your prayers or your expressions of love to God. He cannot endorse your teaching of His word or your spiritual work in anywise. He cannot present your religious exercises with the request that grace be given you (6T 408.2).

Could the curtain be rolled back, could you discern the purposes of God and the judgments that are about to fall upon a doomed world, could you see your own attitude, you would fear and tremble for your own souls and for the souls of your fellow men. Earnest prayers of heart-rending anguish would go up to heaven. You would weep between the porch and the altar, confessing your spiritual blindness and backsliding (6T 408.3).

"Blow the trumpet in Zion, sanctify a fast, call a solemn assembly: gather the people, sanctify the congregation, assemble the elders, gather the children... let the bridegroom go forth of his chamber, and the bride out of her closet. Let the priests, the ministers of the Lord, weep between the porch and the altar, and let them say, Spare Thy people, O Lord, and give not Thine heritage to reproach" Joel 2:15-17 (6T 408.4).

"Turn ye even to Me with all your heart, and with fasting, and with weeping, and with mourning: and rend your heart, and not your garments, and turn unto the Lord your God: for He is gracious and merciful, slow to anger, and of great kindness, and repenteth Him of the evil. Who knoweth if He will return and repent, and leave a blessing behind Him?" Verses 12-14 (6T 409.1).

Many, very many, will be terribly surprised when the Lord shall come suddenly as a thief in the night. Let us watch and pray, lest coming suddenly He find us sleeping. My soul is deeply stirred as I consider how much we ought to do for perishing souls. The prediction of Daniel, "Many shall run to and fro, and knowledge shall be increased," is to be fulfilled in our giving of the warning message; many are to be enlightened regarding the sure word of prophecy (www.egwwritings.org).

Transgression has almost reached its limit. Confusion fills the world, and a great terror is soon to come upon human beings. The end is very near. We who know the truth should be preparing for what is soon to break upon the world as an overwhelming surprise (https://www.egwwritings.org/Lt141-1902.18-21).

When the third angel's message closes, mercy no longer pleads for the guilty inhabitants of the earth. The people of God have accomplished their work. They have received "the latter rain," "the refreshing from the presence of the Lord," and they are prepared for the trying hour before them...The final test has been brought upon the world, and all who have proved themselves loyal to the divine precepts have received "the seal of the living

God." Then Jesus ceases His intercession in the sanctuary above. He lifts His hands and with a loud voice says, "It is done;" and all the angelic host lay off their crowns as He makes the solemn announcement: "He that is unjust, let him be unjust still: and he which is filthy, let him be filthy still: and he that is righteous, let him be righteous still: and he that is holy, let him be holy still." Revelation 22:11. Every case has been decided for life or death. Christ has made the atonement for His people and blotted out their sins...and Jesus is to reign as King of kings and Lord of lords (GC 613.2).

When He leaves the sanctuary, darkness covers the inhabitants of the earth. In that fearful time the righteous must live in the sight of a holy God without an intercessor. The restraint which has been upon the wicked is removed, and Satan has entire control of the finally impenitent. God's long-suffering has ended. The world has rejected His mercy, despised His love, and trampled upon His law. The wicked have passed the boundary of their probation; the Spirit of God, persistently resisted, has been at last withdrawn. Unsheltered by divine grace, they have no protection... *Satan will then plunge the inhabitants of the earth into one great, final trouble.* As the angels of God cease to hold in check the fierce winds of human passion, all the elements of strife will be let loose. The whole world will be involved in ruin (GC 614.1).

Will you receive the gift of God brought by Jesus Christ of everlasting life and hear from the lips of Him who died for you, "Well done, good and faithful servant; ... enter into the joy of thy Lord?" Matthew 25:23. What joy is here spoken of? That joy of seeing souls redeemed in the kingdom of glory. That joy being yours of seeing souls saved through your instrumentality. Will this joy be yours? Will you live an aimless life of self-gratification longer, and in the end reap death and see souls lost through your example and influence who might have been saved? (www.egwwritings.org/, Lt6-1869.14)

Have faith in God. We dishonor Him by our unbelief. Pray, and watch unto prayer. He is touched with the feelings of our infirmities. He is merciful, one who can have compassion on the ignorant, and on them that are out of the way (https://egwwritings.org/, Lt72-1897.16).

We are not to be dependent on the world in a manner to compromise the truth; we are not to be bribed or to attain the world's favor by bowing to the laws of men and setting aside the law of God; we are not to be brought in bondage to the world; and yet we are in the world to live as long as God shall permit, and the Lord has given us a special work to do to save the world (19MR 101.1).

Very many precious opportunities to save souls... have been unheeded and lost. Let us now see how many souls we can save for our Saviour (19MR 4.3).

What is done through the co-operation of men with God is a work that shall never perish, but endure through the eternal ages. He that makes God his wisdom, that grows up into the full stature of a man in Christ Jesus, will stand before kings, before the so-called great men of the world, and show forth the praises of Him who hath called him out of darkness into His marvelous light. Science and literature cannot bring into the darkened mind of men the light which the glorious gospel of the Son of God can bring. The Son of God alone can do the great work of illuminating the soul. No wonder Paul exclaims, "For I am not ashamed of the gospel of Christ; for it is the power of God unto salvation to everyone that believeth." [Romans 1:16.] The gospel of Christ becomes personality in those who believe, and makes them living epistles, known and read of all men. In this way the leaven of godliness passes into the multitude. The heavenly intelligences are able to discern the true elements of greatness in character; for only goodness is esteemed as efficiency with God (CE 97.1).

We are not one-half awake. We have not the power that is essential to the doing of the work that must be done... Now, just now, we must stand in that position where repentance and pardon shall be the striking features of our work. There must be no quarrelling. It is too late to engage with Satan in his work of blinding eyes. It is too late to give heed to seducing spirits and doctrines of devils (AUCR, March 11, 1907 par. 11).

I am instructed to say that when the Holy Spirit gives tongue and utterance, we shall see a work done similar to that done on the day of Pentecost. The representatives of Christ will work intelligently. There will not be found one man here and another there seeking to tear down and destroy (AUCR, March 11, 1907 par. 12).

The Lord is about to do a short and effectual work in the earth. Oh, that our leading workers would realize this, and shun their work of criticizing and forbidding. When the Judge of all the earth shall come to render to every man his reward, those who have laid plans that have hindered the cause of truth will be held responsible for their actions, with all the evil that has resulted therefrom (14MR 137.1).

Before the decree bring forth, before the day pass as the chaff, before the fierce anger of the Lord come upon you, before the day of the Lord's anger come upon you, seek ye the Lord, all ye meek of the earth, which have wrought His judgment; seek righteousness, seek meekness: it may be ye shall be hid in the day of the Lord's anger (AUCR, March 11, 1907 par. 13).

Unless our people arouse to their duties for missions at home, they will be found wanting in the day of God (14MR 137.2).

The cross stands where two roads diverge. One is the path of obedience leading to heaven. The other leads into the broad road, where man can easily go with his burden of sin and corruption, but it leads to perdition. In His sermon on the mount, Christ exhorts His hearers, "Therefore whatsoever ye would that men should do to you, do ye even so to them: for this is the law and the prophets. Enter ye in at the strait gate: for wide is the gate, and broad is the way that leadeth to destruction: and many there be that go in thereat: because strait is the gate, and narrow is the way that leadeth unto life, and few there be that find it." And another time one came to Christ and said, "Lord, are there few that be saved? And He said unto them, Strive to enter in at the strait gate: for many I say unto you shall seek to enter in, and shall not be able" (https://egwwritings.org/).

Take heed to yourselves, lest at any time your hearts be overcharged with surfeiting, and drunkenness, and cares of this life, and so that day come upon you unawares. For as a snare shall it come on all them that dwell on the face of the whole earth. Watch ye therefore, and pray always, that ye may be accounted worthy to escape all these things, and to stand before the Son of man (Luke 21:34-36).

Ponder well the paths your feet are treading. Search your Bibles carefully and prayerfully. Study the waymarks, and inquire diligently whether your feet are in the path leading heavenward, or in the path leading to perdition (1MR 318.1).

Consider the 333 prophecies in the Bible predicting Christ's First Coming. Adrian Rogers has said that if only eight of them were considered (like: Jesus being born at a certain time, at a certain place; His mother being a virgin; babies being killed in an attempt to kill Him; Jesus healing the sick; and then being rejected, crucified, and rising from the dead), if only eight prophecies were merely left to chance, (by the law of probability) it would be impossible for them to happen. Having eight prophecies correct would be like covering the state of Texas with a two-foot pile of silver dollars and then placing a man at a random location tasked with finding a specific coin. He finds it! According to Rogers: Peter Stoner, a statistician, calculated the probability of the 333 prophecies that predicted Christ's First Advent being fulfilled by chance exactly as predicted as astronomically impossible!

Just eight prophecies prove that God's prophetic word is true and trustworthy. Based on getting the 333 prophecies about Christ's First Advent correct, God's accuracy in the past proves that He knows the future and that God has left nothing up to chance. Thus, we are sure that the prophecies about Christ's Second Advent will be fulfilled as well! The truthfulness of Bible prophecy assures us of God's love.

In 1997, God impressed me to study Bible prophecy. I began studying to find out for myself if God is, and if His word is trustworthy. I did not know that millennia before the fact God gave 333 incredible revelations that have been confirmed. God exists! His word is trustworthy!

My quest: To find out what the Bible really said about Christ's Second Advent, I studied Daniel and Revelation. The various churches did not agree. If the Bible is the source of the instruction, how can the churches have contradictions? They relied upon manmade schools of prophetic teaching, tools that are not the Bible. The tools must not replace the Bible. Failing to allow the Bible to explain itself results in prophetic misunderstanding, disputes, and false teachings!

When the Bible spoke for itself, I learned without any doubt that God reveals things that He wants His people to understand. But in spite of diligent Bible study, I did not always get everything right. And though I diligently tried to study with others, folks could not be bothered to study the Bible with me unless every point was infallible. Their focus was not to learn from Bible study, but to teach what they believed. When I enquired about things that they did not believe, rather than looking at the facts and trying to sort it out, folks generally turned from the study. But as prophecy met history, I was able to learn and grow.

The take away is that Bible study is like preparing for a disaster: Folks on a flood plain hope to be ready for floods that may never come. But it is also possible that they may encounter fires, tornadoes, earthquakes, or other disasters that they never imagined. Is it better to prepare for a disaster that may never come or to assume that it is not worthwhile and then to be taken by surprise? Disaster preparedness saves lives! Likewise, studying and heeding Bible prophecy reveals what God wants us to know to saves souls!

Christ's Advent is very near, but time is not the message. What is happening now is the message that must be heard aright! Prepare for the coming conflict between our world and the unseen supernatural world! Self-perpetuating wars, displaced populations, border insecurity, antibiotic resistant epidemics, unparalleled global disasters, rampant drug abuse, violent political wrangling killing innocent people, and the end time loss of our moral compass prophesied to accompany fornicating Babylon's fall. The Time of Trouble will climax with plagues: God's punishment for the rebellion!

> The nations shall rush like the rushing of many waters: but *God* shall rebuke them, and they shall flee far off, and shall be chased as the chaff of the mountains before the wind, and like a rolling thing before the whirlwind (Isaiah 17:13).

> And then shall appear the sign of the Son of man in heaven: and then shall all the tribes of the earth mourn, and they shall see the Son of man coming in the clouds of heaven with power and great glory (Matthew 24:30).

Closing Work

By E. G. White (Review & Herald, October 13, 1904).

We see before us a special work to be done. We are now to pray as never before for the Holy Spirit's guidance. Let us seek the Lord with the whole heart that we may find Him. We have received the light of the three angels' messages; and we need now to come decidedly to the front, and take our position on the side of truth.

The fourteenth chapter of Revelation is a chapter of the deepest interest. This scripture will soon be understood in all its bearings, and the messages given to John the revelator will be repeated with distinct utterance.

The prophecies in the eighteenth of Revelation will soon be fulfilled. During the proclamation of the third angel's message, "another angel" is to "come down from heaven, having great power," and the earth is to be "lighted with his glory." The Spirit of the Lord will so graciously bless consecrated human instrumentalities that men, women, and children will open their lips in praise and thanksgiving, filling the earth with the knowledge of God, and with His unsurpassed glory, as the waters cover the sea.

Those who have held the beginning of their confidence firm unto the end will be wide-awake during the time that the third angel's message is proclaimed with great power. During the loud cry, the church, aided by the providential interpositions of her exalted Lord, will diffuse the knowledge of salvation so abundantly that light will be communicated to every city and town. The earth will be filled with the knowledge of salvation. So abundantly will the renewing Spirit of God have crowned with success the intensely active agencies, that the light of present truth will be seen flashing everywhere.

The saving knowledge of God will accomplish its purifying work on the mind and heart of every believer. The Word declares: "Then will I sprinkle clean water upon you, and ye shall be clean: from all your filthiness, and from all your idols, will I cleanse you. A new heart also will I give you, and a new spirit will I put within you: and I will take away the stony heart out of your flesh, and I will give you an heart of flesh. And I will put my Spirit within you, and cause you to walk in my statutes." This is the descent of the Holy Spirit, sent from God to do its office work. The house of Israel is to be imbued with the Holy Spirit, and baptized with the grace of salvation.

Amid the confusing cries, "Lo, here is Christ! Lo, there is Christ!" will be borne a special testimony, a special message of truth appropriate for this time, which message is to be received, believed, and acted upon. It is the truth, not fanciful ideas, that is efficacious. *The eternal truth of the Word will stand forth free from all seductive errors and spiritualistic interpretations, free from all fancifully drawn, alluring pictures.* Falsehoods will be urged upon the attention of God's people, but the truth is to stand clothed in its beautiful, pure garments. The Word, precious in its holy uplifting influence, is not to be degraded to a level with common, ordinary matters. It is always to remain uncontaminated by the fallacies by which Satan seeks to deceive, if possible, the very elect.

The proclamation of the gospel is the only means in which God can employ human beings as His instrumentalities for the salvation of souls. As men, women, and children proclaim the gospel, the Lord will open the eyes of the blind to see His statutes, and will write upon the hearts of the truly penitent His law. The animating Spirit of God, working through human agencies, leads the believers to be of one mind, one soul, unitedly loving God and keeping His commandments,-- preparing here below for translation.

There have been conflicts, and there will be until in heaven the voice of the Lord is heard, saying, "It is done." And after the redeemed are taken to heaven, God the Father will be glorified in crowning the Lord Jesus, who gave His life a ransom for the world.

Let the work of proclaiming the gospel of Christ be made efficient by the agency of the Holy Spirit. Let not one believer, in the day of trial and proving that has already begun, listen to the devising of the enemy. The living Word is the sword of the Spirit. Mercies and judgments will be sent from heaven. The working of providence will be revealed both in mercies and in judgments.

If we watch and pray and trust God's living Word, we shall gain victories "Watch and pray," Christ said, "that ye enter not into temptation." The day dawns. We must enter each battle with full faith that through Christ we shall be more than conquerors. As faithful watchmen we must diligently guard against the dangers threatening God's people. Other chapters will open before us, and in order to discern their meaning, we shall need keen perception. We are not to be depressed or discouraged, but filled with holy boldness. We are not to be disheartened by the prevalence of sin, or by the difficulties that arise on the right hand and on the left. We must put on the whole armor of God, and stand firm for the right. In the future, Satan's deceptions will assume new forms. False theories, clothed with garments of light, will be presented to God's people. Thus, Satan will try to deceive, if possible, the very elect. Our watchword is to be, "To the law and to the testimony: if they speak not according to this word, it is because there is no light in them." [Isaiah 8:20]

Appendix:

Elihu on the Sabbath

www.en.wikisource.org/wiki/Elihu_on_the_Sabbath
By Benjamin Clark about 1862

This is the love of God, that we keep His commandments (1 John 5:8).

In reviewing the subject of the Sabbath, I design not to follow any previous writer, but simply, plainly, and briefly, to convince sinners of sin, let their profession be what it may. And this I hope and pray may be done without giving offense to those who love the truth more than error; for God has many servants on earth who would gladly exchange error for truth, and many who do exchange their former traditions for the precious and everlasting truths of God as contained in His Word.

Now, the New Testament witnesses to the law and to the prophets; and that book is said to have been written thus: Matthew's Gospel, six years after the resurrection of Christ; Mark's Gospel, ten years after the church commenced; Luke's Gospel, twenty-eight years after; John's Gospel, sixty three years after; the Acts of the Apostles, thirty years after; Romans, First and Second Corinthians, and Galatians, twenty-four years after; Ephesians, Colossians, and Hebrews, twenty-nine years after; to Timothy, Titus, and the second epistle of Peter, thirty years after; the Revelation of John, sixty-one years after; his three epistles, about sixty-five years after the resurrection; and the church had properly commenced. And it is easy for us to understand how these apostles understood and practiced with regard to the Sabbath, and they are the "foundation" next after Christ Himself. Therefore, if there was any such institution known and frequently spoken of in the church as "Sabbath," in those different ages of the church, we can easily know what was then meant by it. Some say, if we keep the seventh day of the week, we shall keep a "Jewish Sabbath." Well, we have no Savior to trust in but Jesus Christ, who was, according to the flesh, a Jew; no other apostles and prophets but Jewish; no other than Jewish Scriptures; and, indeed, Jesus said Himself that "salvation is of the Jews." John 4:22. And what did the writers of the New Testament mean by the words "Sabbath" and "Sabbath day"?

What did Matthew mean in the sixth year of the Christian church? He certainly did not mean the first day of the week, but he meant the day before the first day of the week. See Matthew 28:1. He meant what all other Jewish writers ever meant; viz., "the seventh day is the Sabbath of the Lord thy God." But neither Matthew nor any of the apostles ever told us a word about the Sabbath's being changed from the seventh to the first day of the week. Now, if the Scriptures cannot be broken, but everywhere mean one and the same thing; viz., "the seventh day is the Sabbath of the Lord," then, if ministers contradict this, and say the seventh day is not the Sabbath of the Lord, but the first day of the week is the Sabbath, will they not in this bear witness clearly and positively against themselves, unless they bring forward the chapter and verse where God commanded the Sabbath to be changed?

What did Mark mean by the word "Sabbath"? He meant, also, that the Sabbath was the day before the first day of the week. See Mark 16:1, 2. Surely, if the Sabbath had been changed at the resurrection of Christ, Mark would have known it within ten years afterwards.

What did Luke mean, who wrote twenty-eight years after the resurrection of Christ? He also meant that the Sabbath was the day before the first day of the week; for he says that the women who prepared the ointment rested the Sabbath day, according to the commandment. See Luke 23:56. Thus Luke understood the words "Sabbath day," in the fifty-eighth year of the Christian era, to mean the day immediately preceding the first day of the week.

How did John understand this subject in the sixty-third year of the Christian church? He not only speaks of the Sabbath day as the others did, but he shows plainly that the first day of the week was considered a business day by the disciples after the resurrection. See John 20:1; also, Luke 24:13.

But what did the writer of the Acts of the Apostles mean by the words "Sabbath" and "Sabbath day," thirty years after the Christian church was fully commenced? In writing, he often mentions the Sabbath, and once mentions the first day of the week as meaning quite another thing in plain distinction from the Sabbath. See Acts 13:14, 42, 44; 20:7. The practice of the Jews was then, as it is now, to meet in the synagogue on the seventh day. And again: "The next Sabbath day came almost the whole city together to hear the word of God." He does not say this was the Jewish Sabbath, but the Sabbath day; this was the seventh day; and the first day of the week was not then known as a Sabbath by this writer, because he says the next Sabbath day most all of the Jews and Gentiles came together again. I say there would not have been any "next Sabbath" in the week till the next seventh day. Again, see Acts 16:13. "And on the Sabbath we went out of the city by a riverside, where prayer was wont to be made." He does not say on the Jewish Sabbath, nor on one of the Sabbaths, as though there were two Sabbaths then, but on the Sabbath, i.e., the seventh day, as understood by all Jewish writers of this day. Again, see Acts 17:2, where Paul, as his manner was, went in among the Jews, and three Sabbath days reasoned with them out of the Scriptures.

Thus have I proved that the apostles of Christ understood that one day in the week should be called the Sabbath day; and, further, I have proved that this day was the day before the first day of the week, which is the seventh day; and you cannot deny it, nor by the Scriptures disprove it; consequently, if the apostles of our Lord always called the

Seventh day the Sabbath day, six, ten, twenty-eight, thirty, and sixty-three years after the church was fully commenced, then it must be the Sabbath day now. And every one of the Lord's ministers who calls any other day the Sabbath besides the one so called by the writers of the New Testament, gives it a title which is nowhere found in the Scriptures; for when they say the Sabbath day, they mean something very different from what the New Testament means. It is already proved that the apostles called the seventh day of the week the Sabbath, and the Sabbath day, for many years after the church was fully commenced.

Now we are to show what sin is; and we are not left to guess at it or to suppose it; but we have a given rule to know with certainty what constitutes sin. "By the law," then, "is the knowledge of sin." By what law was the knowledge of sin twenty-four years after the resurrection of Christ? Answer. — The very same law that was given when it was said, "Thou shalt not covet." The law, then, by which sin is known, is the Ten Commandments; and you cannot deny it! This law says, "The seventh day is the Sabbath of the Lord thy God: in it thou shalt not do any work, thou, nor thy son, nor thy daughter, thy manservant, nor thy maidservant, nor thy cattle, nor thy stranger that is within thy gates: for in six days the Lord made heaven and earth, the sea, and all that in them is, and rested the seventh day: wherefore the Lord blessed the Sabbath day, and hallowed it." See Exodus 20:10, 11. Now, until this law is altered or abrogated (and Christ says He came not "to destroy the law") by the same power that enacted it, a willful transgression of it is a willful sin, let your profession be what it may; for "sin is the transgression of the law." He that offends in one point, or in one of these commandments, is guilty of all, i.e., he is a transgressor of the law, a sinner in the sight of God. But a regenerated soul, a true-hearted Christian, says with Paul: "I delight in the law of God after the inward man." See Romans 7:22. "The law is holy, and the commandment holy, and just, and good." See Romans 7:12. And any person, who is not willing to keep the commandments of God, when plainly understood, has still a carnal mind, which "is not subject to the law of God, neither indeed can be." See Romans 8:7.

Will you say this is judging too hard? Or, "This is an hard saying; who can hear it?" I wish to judge no man; but the word that the Lord has spoken, the same shall judge you in the last day. See John 12:48. "As many as have sinned in the law shall be judged by the law; ...in the day when God shall judge the secrets of men by Jesus Christ according to my gospel." See Romans 2:12-16. Then those who shall hold the truth in unrighteousness, those who pretend to keep the law differently from what God appointed it, those who, in fact, lay aside the commandments of God (the fourth or any other command) and teach for doctrine the commandments of men (the observance of the first day instead of the seventh), such, the Word says, are vain worshipers. See Mark 7:7.

But you say, it makes no difference which day is kept or called the Sabbath day, provided we keep one seventh part of the time! This is not correct, because God never said so. God is not to be mocked in this way. He has been very good and kind to make the Sabbath for man, to appoint the day, and the particular time of the day when the Sabbath is to commence and when it is to end; it is the seventh day in order from the creation — the seventh day in the creation; and He said, "From even unto even, shall ye celebrate your Sabbath" (see Leviticus 23:32); as the evening and the morning were reckoned for the day. God did not leave this subject undecided, so that His people would appoint different days, and then everyone call his own the Sabbath day. But God blessed and sanctified the seventh day, and proved that particular day to be designated by Him, in the face and eyes of about six hundred thousand witnesses, by a miracle directly from heaven, in withholding the manna on that day, and in giving the food for that day on the day before; and it cannot be denied or disproved.

Again, you ask, How shall we know which is the seventh day? I answer, Do you wish to know? Then ask the Jews; for

God has committed the lively oracles to them, and then scattered them among the nations. Do you know when the first day of the week comes? Well, the Sabbath is always the day before the first day of the week. See Matthew 28:1. But you may say, Do not the majority of honest-hearted Christians keep the first day of the week? And have they not for centuries done common labor on the seventh day, and observed the first in obedience to the fourth command, and still been honest in their motives, and living Christians? I answer, "What is that to us, so long as the true light of the Sabbath did not come to their minds?"

Now, we certainly know what sin is, not by what popular writers say — not by the popular traditions of our fathers — not altogether by our feelings — but by the law of God is this knowledge; for sin is the transgression of the law; and all who have the law of God have an infallible and everlasting rule to know what sin is. Art thou a willful transgressor of the law of God? Then by the law is the knowledge that thou art a willful sinner before God. But if thou art an ignorant transgressor of the law of God, then by the law is the knowledge that thou art an ignorant sinner before God. To say nothing of presumptuous sin, I say, If thou hast ignorantly sinned, then repent and reform, and God will heal you. See Lev. 4:2, 13.

By the law of God, then, is the clear knowledge of sin. I speak to you, Protestants, who keep the Sunday, a day formerly dedicated to the worship of the sun by the pagans, and afterwards brought into the Church by Constantine and Roman Catholics, and called the Christian Sabbath, a name never known for the first day of the week by any of the writers of the New Testament. I speak to you, Protestants, and ask you if you have any given rule to know what sin is. Have you any certain rule to know whether Roman Catholics sin or not, in bowing down to images? They say they do not sin! You say you know they do sin. But how do you know it is sin to bow down to images, when they say it is not sin? Answer— By the law, you say, you know this is sin, and you know it by no other rule; for you "had not known sin, but by the law." Well, by the same rule, I know what sin is. You say it is not sin to work and do common labor on the seventh day. But we know, not by your assertion, but by the law, whether you sin or not. You say you know by the law that it is sin to bow down to images. I say (by your own rule), I know by the law that it is sin to do common labor on the seventh day; and you cannot deny it. And, if you know it is the duty of Roman Catholics to repent of their sins for transgressing the second command, then I know it is also your duty to repent of your sins for transgressing the fourth command. He who said, "Thou shalt not kill," "Thou shalt not steal," "Thou shalt not bow down thyself to them [images], nor serve them," etc., also said, "The seventh day is the Sabbath."

Can you not see the weakness of the argument; viz., that one seventh part of time was meant in the law, without regard to any particular day? In this you make the commandments of God of no effect through your tradition. Yea, you make void the part of the command which says, "The seventh day is the Sabbath of the Lord thy God." We read, not that the Lord blessed the seventh part of time or the Sabbath institution, as you say, but the seventh day in particular. Why do you wish to take out and make void this part of the fourth command, when Christ has said, "Till heaven and earth pass, one jot or one tittle shall in nowise pass from the law"? See Matthew 5:18. It was just as necessary that the particular day should be designated as it was that there should be a Sabbath made for man. It would not have been according to divine wisdom to say, Thou shalt keep one seventh part of time, or one day in seven, because this would have left mankind in as much confusion as your theory could make them! One might have kept one day, another the next, until seven Sabbaths were kept in one family. Thus, so much for the seventh part of time theory.

Suppose a parent should command his child to do a certain piece of labor on a certain day, and that the child should, without any just cause, neglect to perform the labor on the day specified, and should perform it on the next day.

Would this show any respect for the authority of the parent? Or would the parent approve such conduct in his child? You must say, No. Or, if a governor should command all the military to do duty two days in the year, and leave each one to select his own days, there would be as much wisdom in this as in the seventh part of time for the Sabbath of the Lord. God is not; the author of confusion, but of order; while the theory of one seventh part of time, or one whole day in seven, instead of the seventh day, impeaches the divine wisdom, and makes God the author of confusion. Thus, the theory, not the law of God, leads to anarchy and confusion, and to the observance of no Sabbath; and it cannot be denied. What reasonable objection have you to the law of God? What fault can you find with it just as it stands? Have you wisdom enough to change it for the "better?" "The law of the Lord is perfect, converting the soul." See Psalm 19:7. Yea, it is so perfect that it has already converted the souls of many, even from the doctrines and commandments of men, to keep the Sabbath of the Lord, and I trust it will convert many more; because "the statutes of the Lord are right, rejoicing the heart: the commandment of the Lord is pure, enlightening the eyes.... More to be desired are they than gold, yea, than much fine gold: sweeter also than honey and the honeycomb." Verses 8-10. "Wherefore the law is holy, and the commandment holy, and just, and good.... For I [Paul] delight in the law of God after the inward man." See Romans 7:1222.

Reader, dost thou delight in the law of God after the inward man? If not, thy soul should be converted, by praying for the law of God to be put into thy heart, and written in thy mind. But, if the law of God is already thy delight, then why not be reconciled to it? Why not be subject to it just as it stands? Why wish to make void one jot or tittle of it? I do not present the law for justification; but as a perfect rule of right in this life; first, between man and his Creator; secondly, between man and his fellow man. "Whosoever therefore shall break one of these least commandments, and shall teach men so, he shall be called the least in the kingdom of heaven:

but whosoever shall do and teach them, the same shall be called great in the kingdom of heaven." See Matthew 5:19.

The Westminster divines found contradicting the writer of the Acts of the Apostles! These divines say, "From the beginning of the world to the resurrection of Christ, God appointed the seventh day of the week to be the weekly Sabbath, and the first day of the week ever since, to continue to the end of the world, which is the Christian Sabbath."

1. Luke (the writer of the Acts of the Apostles) says (Acts 13:14), Paul and his company went into a synagogue of the Jews on the Sabbath day; this was, according to our account, A. D. 45, and twelve years after the resurrection of Christ. Luke says this was on the Sabbath day then, at that time. But the divines say this was not on the Sabbath day at that time, but on Saturday, and that the seventh day was not then the Sabbath, neither had been for twelve years. Thus, they contradict Luke plainly and pointedly.

2. Luke says (Acts 13:42, 44) that "when the Jews were gone out of the synagogue, the Gentiles besought that these words [of the gospel] might be preached to them the next Sabbath." "And the next Sabbath day came almost the whole city together to hear the word of God." This, Luke says, was on the Sabbath day at that time, twelve years after the resurrection. But the divines say that it was not on the Sabbath at that time; for Sunday had been the Sabbath for twelve years.

3. Luke says (Acts 16:13): "And on the Sabbath we went out of the city by a riverside, where prayer was wont to be made;" A. D. 53, twenty years after the resurrection, and ten years before the Acts of the Apostles was written. This, Luke says, was actually on the Sabbath day at that time; but the divines contradict him, saying this was not the Sabbath at

that time, but on Saturday; for the seventh day was not then the Sabbath, neither had been for twenty years — never since the resurrection of Christ! Thus, they contradict Luke again; for all admit that Luke always called the seventh day, the day the Jews met in their synagogue, the Sabbath, in the Acts of the Apostles.

4. Luke says (Acts 17:2-4) Paul, at Thessalonica, "as his manner was," went into a synagogue of the Jews, and so preached Christ and the resurrection three Sabbath days that some Jews and a great multitude of the gentiles believed. This was twenty years after the resurrection of Christ. This, Luke says, was on three Sabbath days then, at that time. But the divines deny this also, because they say that the Sabbath had "been changed from the seventh to the first day of the week twenty years before." Thus, they give Luke the lie.

5. Luke says (Acts 18:3, 4) Paul, at Corinth, labored with his hands, as tentmaker (on the other days, as we should understand), but "reasoned in the synagogue every Sabbath, and persuaded the Jews and the Greeks." This was A. D. 54, twenty-one years after the resurrection of Christ, and nine years before the Acts of the Apostles was written. This, Luke said, or wrote, A. D. 63, the thirtieth year after the resurrection, and the thirtieth year of the Christian church that this preaching of Paul was on every Sabbath; that is, on every seventh day, the same day that the Jews always met in their synagogue for worship. This is plain, pointed, and positive proof that the seventh day was the Sabbath, at least thirty years after the resurrection of Christ; for Luke testified again and again that those meetings of the Jews and gentiles were held on the Sabbath; and if Luke was a

Christian, then the seventh day was the Christian Sabbath thirty years after the resurrection, the Westminster divines to the contrary notwithstanding. And if the seventh day was the Sabbath thirty years after the resurrection of Christ, as Luke says it was, then it is the Sabbath now; for no man, or body of men, have had any lawful right to alter or change this command of God since A. D. 63. But we find not one word in favor of the idea, not even the least hint or allusion in all the New Testament that the first day of the week was ever so much as thought of as a Christian Sabbath by any of the apostles while they lived. And you must give it up; yea, and you will give it up, if you search the Scriptures carefully and prayerfully on this subject, and if you have a spirit of discernment, and are willing to forsake error for truth, and if you are an honest Christian in the sight of God.

Now, the Scriptures are able to make one wise unto salvation, through faith in Jesus Christ; then why need I stop to examine all the various doctrines of popes, councils, and fathers, when, in searching, I should find pope against pope, council against council, and fathers against fathers? This would be like two companies fighting at great distance, with small arms. But if we wish to come to close action, let us take the armor of truth, which will most assuredly prevail; and the closer the action, the sooner the victory will be won on the side of truth.

Now, my dear reader, if you will take the Scriptures and search them as above requested, then you will find the following valuable treasures of knowledge among the many therein contained:

1. You will find Christ Himself saying, "The Sabbath was made for man," and that it was made when the first seven days were made, before man had sinned. The Sabbath was thus made not for the Jews in

particular, but as a gift of God to man, i.e., to mankind universally, of all nations and of all ages of the world.

2.   You will find that before the law was given at Mt. Sinai, this was a law and a commandment (Exodus 16); that it was also written by the finger of God, with the "lively oracles," which God committed to the Jews to give to us; that this law, by which is the clear knowledge of sin, is an infallible and everlasting rule by which, to know what is sin, and what is not sin; that sin is the transgression of the law; and that to act against it, or to do things contrary to it, is sin; but "where no law is, there is no transgression;" that this law Christ came not to destroy, abrogate, or make void; that the law is holy, and just, and good; and that Christians delight in it. And as Paul had not "known lust, except the law had said, Thou shalt not covet," so we had not known which day of the week was the Sabbath, except the law had said, "The seventh day is the Sabbath of the Lord thy God." Now, we know by the law that this is the Sabbath, without the help of commentators.

3. You can find that the resurrection of our Saviour has nothing to do with changing the Sabbath, any more than His birth, His death, or His ascension had. Whether He was risen near the end of the Sabbath, or some time before the common time of beginning the first-day sabbath, so-called, has nothing to do with altering one jot or one tittle of the law of God.

4.   You can find that the common reasonings of men, that Christ frequently met with His disciples on the first day of the week after His resurrection more than on other days, are false and without foundation; that He went with two of them to Emmaus, about seven and a half miles, and returned to Jerusalem,

which would plainly show that He did not regard that day as a Sabbath; that He met with His disciples in the evening, which must have been after the beginning of the second day of the week (see Genesis 1:8), when they were met, but not to celebrate the resurrection, as false reasoners pretend; that He met with them again "after eight days," i.e. , near the middle of the next week; and again they were together fishing, so that the fishing day would prove a Sabbath, as much as either of the first two visits.

5. You can find that Luke had not forgotten the distinction between the "first day of the week" and "the Sabbath day" (Acts 20:7), in his recording the meeting of the disciples to break bread on that day; and that this is the only time the first day of the week is mentioned in all the Acts of the Apostles; and it is the only notice of Paul's preaching on that particular day, or rather, evening, and that on a particular occasion; viz., in order to be "ready to depart on the morrow;" that this one instance of the first day's being mentioned proves that it was not the Sabbath, and that the many meetings of the Jews and gentiles, believers and unbelievers, where Paul preached "every Sabbath," certainly did not occur on the first day of the week.

6. You may find that Paul, in giving orders to some of the churches to lay by themselves in store something according as God had prospered them, on the first day of the week for the poor saints at Jerusalem (1 Corinthians 16:2), does not prove that to be the Sabbath day, but that it was not the Sabbath day, nor suitable to a Sabbath day's work; but rather as an offering to the Lord of "the first ripe fruits of their increase;" to be the first business attended to in the week, to reckon up their earnings and incomes, and

devote a part of the same, and lay it by itself, so that it would be ready when Paul came. This was a good calculation for the first business of the week.

7. You can find that as there is no law of God against doing common labor on the first day of the week, therefore it is no sin or transgression of any law other than the laws and commandments of men.

8. You can find that the Savior said to His disciples, "If ye love Me, keep My commandments." Again, "He that hath My commandments, and keepeth them, he it is that loveth Me: and he that loveth Me shall be loved of My Father, and I will love him, and will manifest Myself to him." Again, "Jesus answered and said unto him [Judas, not Iscariot], If a man love Me, he will keep My words: and My Father will love him, and We will come unto him, and make Our abode with him."

Now, my dear reader, if you neglect or refuse to obey this fourth command of the Decalogue, are you not left without excuse? And you can plead nothing in extenuation of your neglect. "For God shall bring every work into judgment, with every secret thing, whether it be good or whether it be evil."

www.ingramcontent.com/pod-product-compliance
Lightning Source LLC
Chambersburg PA
CBHW051840090426
42736CB00011B/1900